June 22, :

Patti Hamilton WVACo

MM   A.C.

Melissa Garretson CFJA

9 8 7 6 5 4 3 2 1

First Edition

(c) 2013 by West Virginia Association of Counties.

ISBN 978-1-4675-5777-1

Printed in the United States

Design and Layout by The Walkabout Company, LLC
P.O. Box 3116, Wheeling, WV 26003
www.gowalkabout.com

This edition is published by:
Black Tie Press
A Division of Black Tie Productions, Inc.
P.O. Box 14527
Cincinnati, Ohio 45250
www.blacktieinc.com

A Project of the West Virginia Association of Counties
A Walkabout Company Publication

Living Monuments:
The Courthouses
of West Virginia

A Project of the West Virginia Association of Counties

Authors

Debra Warmuth
Richard Warmuth

Table of Contents

The Story of the Book

Once, when I was in college, my late father suggested that it would be a good project to travel the state and record each monument. He said that they not only represented important events in our collective history, they also helped us understand who we are as a people. It's been many years since we had that conversation, but I never forgot it. Finally, the time was right and the opportunity to search out all the monuments presented itself. The idea of a monument had evolved over those years to refocus on the grandest monument of all - one that is not just of stone or bronze, rather it is a living one. It continues to grow and evolve. It is the courthouse - a cornerstone of our democracy.

Our republic depends on a matrix of governments to make it all work - a complex machine in which all the parts are responsible to the greater whole. There is no other place where this is more apparent than at the county level. Democracy requires a certain amount of interaction and accountability to survive generation to generation. It is most evident with the elected officials and workers that each day enter the county courthouse to perform their tasks in the public trust. The courthouse is probably the one place where a citizen can freely enter, ask questions, get answers, and generally interact with government.

In creating this book, we had the great fortune to travel to each county in the state, often more than once. This afforded us the opportunity to meet and talk with the people that actually work in the courthouses. Perhaps the overarching quality that we observed is that everyone we met was welcoming and genuinely friendly. They were quite proud of their courthouse, usually taking time to point out interesting features or convey some of the history associated with their part of the state. While we certainly bear a prejudice in favor of our courthouses, it's the people that you meet inside that most often makes the journey a memorable and satisfying experience.

As you continue though the pages, in addition to exterior pictures, there are photos of each courtroom and some of the interior details that are not often enjoyed by the public. Each courthouse is unique. Some are magnificent public buildings on a grand scale. There are splendid towers piercing the sky and detailed stonework that would be equally at home on a medieval castle. There are also more modest buildings - modern in design with clean lines and lower profiles. Regardless of the design or period of origin, they all have one thing in common - they are the repositories of our lives - wills, deeds, marriages, births and deaths. The documentation that marks life in our communities is all there.

We found a county clerk, with artistic skill, that did the lettering on the office doors to save money - really nice work. Burgers and potato salad were consumed as we were welcomed at one courthouse. Personal tours were conducted to be sure we saw all the significant details and heard all the stories - our thanks. Original artwork decorated many walls. Veterans will never be forgotten - thanks to our courthouses. We saw monuments and read plaques, even one to a Medal of Honor recipient that served with the 7th Cavalry and survived the Battle of the Little Big Horn in 1876.

We would like to extend our gratitude to the West Virginia Association of Counties for the opportunity to create this little slice of time and help bring attention to our 55 counties and their courthouses. Our thanks also goes to all those who supported our efforts and the county officials and employees that made our work possible, and an enjoyable experience.

Our best advice - read the book, travel the state and see for yourself. The history, the color, the sense of who we are - it is a fantastic journey.

The Authors

County courthouses are the frameworks that hold the offices of hundreds of employees across the State. They serve as the focal point for communities, bringing business people, tourists, historians, and citizens to a common ground. They are the ever present symbols of fundamental democracy. They are our history - the legacy of freedom that is passed generation to generation. They are theaters of high drama played out in a courtroom. They hold the records of our lives - from the distant past to the present - ready to communicate that information to the future. They are impressive, beautiful examples of architectural style. All of this and much more is true of West Virginia's County Courthouses.

The West Virginia Association of Counties is proud to be a part of the first large, full-color publication to feature West Virginia's Courthouses, in honor of the State's Sesquicentennial in 2013. As our state celebrates its first 150 years, it is appropriate to commemorate the past while planning for the future - to embrace our heritage and learn how to best to build our future. The history, present, and the future of our Counties and our State are intertwined in our Courthouses through their style of architecture, notable events, and to the activity that takes place within, to maintain and improve the delivery of county government responsibilities and services to our citizens.

We invite you to enjoy the beautiful photographs, the tradition, and the tales that our Courthouses tell. From trials to taxes, elections to enforcement of laws, our West Virginia Courthouses are an integral part of our lives and are ready to meet the challenges of the next 150 years.

Patricia L Hamilton, CAE
Executive Director
West Virginia Association of Counties

6

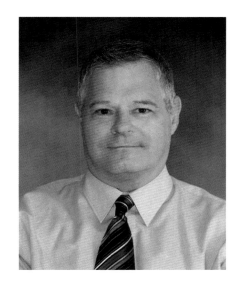

By their very nature, courthouses are centers. They are obviously centers of government and of commerce, especially in rural counties. Courthouses are often central geographic sites in a community. In short, they are showcases.

In 2001, the West Virginia Legislature created the Courthouse Facilities Improvement Authority. Its goals were to create funding to make certain West Virginia's courthouses remained the showcases they rightly should be. The legislation recognized the great expense in remodeling and maintaining courthouses, and that West Virginia's counties could not go it alone. The Legislature also recognized that the state had an interest in the preservation of our courthouses.

Since its creation, the Authority has given on average Two Million Dollars a year to counties. These funds assist in necessary repairs and renovations to improve safety, access, and to protect courthouses from damage and destruction. I'm proud to be a part of a diverse group of state and county officials who make the tough decisions of funding among numerous valid requests. I wish we could fund more projects.

This book, and the documentary upon which it is based, are showcases of our showcases. We often come into the courthouse to pay our taxes, or file a deed. We need to take the time to appreciate the architecture and construction of the courthouse. Much of the architecture reflects the county itself. Many were built with limited funds, but with limitless dedication of local officials to make their courthouses the centers of their county's attention. Think of the tough financial and transportation issues counties faced when building many courthouses. Counties persevered and the results are fifty-five fine examples of their committment.

I hope this book helps you see more than history and architecture. May it also bring understanding and appreciation of the hard work and dedication which went into the construction and maintenance of our courthouses. We hope you will find a renewed interest in maintaining and improving these wonderful centers of government. The next time you visit your courthouse to pay your taxes or file a deed, look up and around. You will gain a new perspective of a jewel right in your own backyard.

W. Richard Staton
Prosecuting Attorney
Wyoming County

Chairman and Founder
WV Courthouse Facilities Improvement Authority

The Facts

National Reputation
State Insight
Client Focus

Jackson Kelly is committed to supporting the state and communities that have been our home for nearly two centuries. From administrative matters to jury trials and appellate advocacy, to complex infrastructure and economic development financing, Jackson Kelly lawyers have the experience you need.

Benchmark: Litigation 2011 – Best Commercial and Financial Litigators in the United States: Ranked among the "highly recommended" firms.

2013 edition of The Best Lawyers in America®
(copyright 2012 by Woodward/White, Inc., of Aiken, S.C.)
Sixty-three Jackson Kelly lawyers listed.
Nine lawyers listed as "Lawyer of the Year"

Jackson Kelly attorneys hold membership in the National Association of Bond Lawyers and have been recognized by publications such as Woodward/White's *The Best Lawyers in America®*, Chambers USA and Super Lawyers.

www.silling.com

SILLING
ARCHITECTS + PLANNERS

"THESE OLD BUILDINGS DO NOT BELONG TO US ONLY...THEY HAVE BELONGED TO OUR FOREFATHERS AND THEY WILL BELONG TO OUR DESCENDANTS UNLESS WE PLAY THEM FALSE. THEY ARE NOT...OUR PROPERTY, TO DO AS WE LIKE WITH. WE ARE ONLY TRUSTEES FOR THOSE THAT COME AFTER US." WILLIAM MORRIS (1889)

405 Capitol Street, Upper Atrium
Charleston, West Virginia 25301
p 304.346.0565   f 304.346.1522

9

West Virginia's First Member Owned Public Entity Risk Pool

39 County Commissions

70 County Authorities

WWW.WVRISK.ORG
(888)822-6772

Gold Level Sponsors

Chesapeake Energy
Oklahoma City, OK
www.chk.com

West Virginia Courthouse Facilities
Improvement Authority
2003 Quarrier Street
Charleston, WV 25311
www.cfia.wv.gov

Pocahontas Land Corporation
800 Princeton Avenue
Bluefield, WV 24701
www.nscorp.com

The Bell Law Firm PLLC

The Bell Law Firm PLLC
30 Capitol Street
Charleston, WV 25301
www.belllaw.com

ANGA
701 8th Street, NW
Suite 800
Washington, DC 20001
www.anga.us

Robinson and McElwee
700 Virginia Street
400 Fifth Third Center
Charleston, WV 25301
www.ramlaw.com

Mylan Inc.
1500 Corporate Drive
Canonsburg, PA 15317
www.mylan.com

ZMM
222 Lee Street West
Charleston, WV 25302
www.zmm.com

Software Systems, Inc.
23 South University Avenue
Morgantown, WV
www.softwaresystems.com

Essays

The County Courthouse
Michael Workman, Ph.D.

Why Rehabilitate A Courthouse?
Michael Gioulis

The County Courthouse
Michael Workman, Ph.D

Ask a group of West Virginians where they are from, and chances are most will reply with the name of their home county. West Virginia is one of the most rural states, and Mountaineers think of their counties as home in the same way that urban Americans identify with their cities or neighborhoods. The county is the unit of government to which West Virginians feel most closely attached.[1] They provide a broad array of services, from recording vital information to dispensing justice. Since the voters of each county elect their officials - commissioners, county clerk, circuit clerk, prosecuting attorney, sheriff, assessor, surveyor of lands - who provide these services, county governments are not only the most immediate arm of government, they are also the most democratic.

Home for county government is the courthouse. Located at the county seat, the courthouse is the place where county government conducts business - where one can observe local democracy in action. The courthouse is also a center of community life - often the venue for Independence Day, Memorial Day, and Veteran's Day ceremonies. It is the place where political campaigns are started, where votes are counted following an election, and where citizens gather to exercise their First Amendment rights of expression and protest. The courthouse serves to promote the civic ideals critical for the continuance of our Republic.

The courthouse is usually the most elaborate and beautiful building in the county. Cherished by communities and used as a landmark,[2] the courthouses are architectural monuments which "stand as symbols of democracy and freedom and represent a community's wealth, pride and aspirations."[3] The architectural styles reflected in West Virginia's courthouses vary dramatically. This wonderful diversity is a result of a number of factors: the period of construction, the wealth of the county, the knowledge and attitude of those who commissioned the buildings, and the imagination and vision of their architects. They come in a variety of styles: Georgian, Federal, Greek Revival, Gothic Revival, Romanesque Revival, Italianate, Colonial Revival, Neo-Classical Revival, Beaux Arts, Richardsonian Romanesque, Art Deco and Modern. Courthouses are often historic buildings that are listed on the National Register of Historic Places, the national honor roll of buildings and sites maintained by the National Park Service. Significant because of their architectural features and/or connection to important historic events, many courthouses retain original features appropriate to their styles. And, unlike many monuments that are set aside for observation and ceremony, our courthouses teem with activity. They are living monuments that deserve to be preserved in their entire splendor as tangible links to our state's history.

The origins of our county government can be traced back to our mother state, the Commonwealth of Virginia, which inherited it from England. The English system dates to that shrouded period near the end of the first millennium, when English kings divided their realm into districts called shires to maintain royal power. The term shire is largely anachronistic today, though it survives in the name of one West Virginia county, Hampshire. The shire was simply a mechanism for projecting royal power to distant places: all of its authority was derived from the king. An earl, usually a large landholder, was appointed by the king to exercise authority in his name. The shire also had a shire court composed of local landholders and a shire-reeve (the origin of our modern sheriff), who served as president of the shire court, tax collector, and steward of the royal estates. The Norman conquest of England in 1066 brought changes to the shire system. The name itself disappeared, replaced by the French term comte, from which the term county is derived. Earls, whose power the Normans feared, became a title of nobility, rather than a position of power. The sheriff arose as the chief county official. Further changes were made during the reign of King Edward III (1327-1377). Edward created a new officer, justice of the peace, to assume some of the executive powers of the sheriff. Each county had at least one; some had as many as sixty. Later, the offices of coroner and constable were created as county officials. Thus, even before Columbus discovered America, two of the major characteristics of the modern county system already had been put in place: 1) the county as a purely administrative unit, an agency of the state lacking sovereignty; and 2) the plural nature of the county executive.[4]

The county system of local government came to America, and, like so many English customs and institutions, was adapted to new conditions. Over time it changed. In Virginia, after tobacco was discovered as the road to wealth, the plantation system was put into place during the first half of the seventeenth century. The population was dispersed among scattered estates and no real towns developed. The natural unit of local government to serve such large, rural areas was the English county. Accordingly, in 1634, eight counties were created. Their number was increased from time to time as the population increased and settlers surged westward. Meanwhile, the county system was modified dramatically in New England, where closely-knit towns developed. Counties were created, but town governments emerged as far more powerful and important. Something of a mixed, or hybrid, system of local government developed in Pennsylvania. By the middle of the eighteenth century, Virginia's strong county system had become the norm in the southern colonies, New England's strong town/weak county system had been adopted in the North, and Pennsylvania's mixed system had become the pattern for the middle colonies.[5]

The county court emerged as the most important governing body in rural Virginia. It was composed of justices of the peace, varying in number from eight to eighteen. The county court met monthly, and despite its name, exercised legislative and executive, as well as judicial functions. Justices were appointed by Virginia's governor from the most illustrious men of the county. They served indefinite terms, and, theoretically could be removed by the governor. However, it became common practice for new governors to re-appoint sitting members of the court. When a vacancy arose, governors followed the practice of appointing new members from the recommendations of sitting members. This made the court a closed, self-perpetuating--and conservative--institution. The principal duty of the county court was to hear and decide cases, both civil and criminal. In some cases, a petit jury was used to settle questions of fact, but the opinions of the majority of the court were law.

The court performed a variety of other duties, including authorizing and repairing roads and bridges, maintaining public buildings, laying the county levy and assessing property. Among its other powers, the county court: nominated inspectors of tobacco, granted divorces, regulated the relations of the whites to the Indians, tried cases of piracy, erected ducking-stools, pillories, whipping posts and stocks, appointed collectors of county levies, and regulated the relation of master to slave.[6]

As with the county court, the counties of colonial Virginia were governed by several lesser officers, none of whom were elected by the people. The sheriff was the most important. Invariably, he was a former justice, recommended by his peers for this remunerative position held for a one-year term. The sheriff executed court orders, made arrests, served legal papers, and acted as the general peace officer of the county. He could also be called upon to collect taxes, and was the regular county jailer. In fact, his duties were not very different from those of the present-day sheriff.[7]

In addition to the sheriff, constables were appointed by the county court to enforce law and order in each of the county's precincts. The county clerk, appointed by the secretary of state of the colony, recorded and cared for all county records. The clerk was paid on the fee basis, and his office could be lucrative. He shared the loot with an officer of the Commonwealth, the secretary of state. It was not until 1711 that prosecuting attorneys were appointed for the counties. Prior to that, the persons who reported the crime to the court had the responsibility of prosecuting the case; these informers were given one-half of all fines imposed. The potential for abuse of this system is obvious, and explains its reform. Another county official, who was of considerable importance in frontier counties, was the county lieutenant. Commonly styled "Colonel," and usually coming from gentry (landed proprietors), he was commander-in-chief of the armed forces of the county, the militia.[8]

Virginia's system of local government made its way across the Allegheny Mountains during the eighteenth and nineteenth centuries as settlers pushed their way into the western part of the Commonwealth. All of West Virginia's counties descend from two giant counties of Virginia, Frederick and Augusta, created in 1743 and 1745, respectively, and named for the prince and princess of Wales. These counties were carved into smaller units as settlers demanded access to government services: the rule-of-thumb was that the county should be small enough to require no more than a day-trip for settlers to conduct business at the county seat and return home. Two of West Virginia's counties were created during the colonial era: Hampshire, formed in 1754, and Berkeley, created in 1772. Ohio and Monongalia were created in 1776, the year of American independence.[9]

    Most of West Virginia's counties were created during the nineteenth century, especially in the two or three decades before the Civil War. Named for important political figures of the time, their names provide an interesting glimpse of our history. For example, Jackson County was formed in 1831 and named for the sitting president, Andrew Jackson. Wirt County, organized in 1848, was named for William Wirt, a politician, lawyer and author from Maryland and Virginia who was a candidate for president in 1832 on the anti-Masonic party ticket. Marquis de Lafayette, who served in the Continental Army under General Washington and promoted liberal democracy in revolutionary France, was the namesake for Fayette County, which was organized in 1831. Even more interesting is the fact that several of our standing courthouses date to the ante-bellum period and reflect architectural styles popular at that time. Brooke County's courthouse at Wellsburg and the Jefferson County courthouse at Charlestown date to 1849 and 1836, respectively, the heyday of Jacksonian democracy. Both were built in the Greek Revival style, reflecting America's fascination with ancient Greece and its democratic institutions.

    Just as national politics during the ante-bellum period was dominated by sectional rivalry between the North and the South, Virginia was beset with a sectionalism that divided East and West. The planter elite and slavery dominated politics in the tidewater region, while west of the Blue Ridge, the region held few slaves and most of its population were farmers or small-town professionals who looked to commerce and industry as the path to progress. Politicians from the two sections clashed on nearly every issue. The westerners wanted public education, internal improvements (turnpikes, river improvement and railroads), and a more democratic political system. At the local level, western reformers wanted to overthrow the county court system, which they criticized as undemocratic and prone to promote favoritism and corruption. They wished to replace appointed county officials with ones elected by the people.

    Finally, in 1851 as the profitability of eastern plantations declined and the population of western Virginia increased, the Virginia constitution was reformed by a special convention. Significant concessions were made to the West in regard to representation in the General Assembly and suffrage. Significantly, the constitution provided for the popular election of all county officials, including justices of the peace. This 1851 Reform Constitution reflected the triumph of Jacksonian democracy in America. Jacksonians believed in thwarting any consolidation of power at the local level by separating governmental functions among a number of offices, and setting term limits that provided for frequent elections. The new, more democratic, Constitution, made significant progress toward resolving sectional differences. In fact, the Shenandoah Valley counties were largely reconciled to the Richmond government. But, it was not enough to bind the transmontane counties during the coming crisis of the Civil War.

    The war itself led to divided loyalties within the new state and tore many counties apart, leaving legacies that endure today. Not only was the state of West Virginia created in dramatic fashion with a revolution, but the system of county government was also revolutionized - at least for a few years.

    One county that eventually became part of the new state, Jefferson, was the scene of perhaps the most pivotal event leading up to the Civil War: John Brown's Harper's Ferry raid. Charged with murder, conspiracy to incite a slave rebellion, and, by the 1819 statute, high treason against the Commonwealth of Virginia, he was tried in the Jefferson County courthouse at Charlestown. The week-long trial resulted in Brown being found guilty on all three counts: he was sentenced to be hanged in public on December 2, 1859.[10] He was executed in Charlestown, near the courthouse, after writing his famous prediction: *"I, John Brown, am now quite certain that the crimes of this guilty land will never be purged away but with blood..."*. Few have been as accurate as the war would eventually claim the lives of over 620,000.

    The war disrupted nearly every county government south of the northern panhandle. Fayette County's courthouse was destroyed by Union troops in 1861. Fueled by the war's tension, Charles Town and Shepherdstown vied for control of the Jefferson county seat.

Cabell County's seat was moved from Barboursville to Guyandotte, because the former had been taken over by Confederates in 1863. Mercer County's second courthouse at Princeton was destroyed by Confederates in 1862; the long-standing competition between Concord Church (Athens) and Princeton for control of the county seat, which continued until 1874, was rooted in Civil War animosities.[11]

As one would expect, the constitution of the new state broke dramatically with Virginia's practice, particularly in regard to the sections dealing with local government. The state's founding fathers were determined to limit the power of the county courts, which, for the most part, had remained loyal to Virginia during the war. Reflecting the influence of New England, the 1863 Constitution provided for governmental sub-units within the counties called townships. Each county was divided into no less than three and no more than ten townships. At a yearly township meeting, a variation on the New England town meeting, voters were to transact township business and elect a supervisor, clerk, surveyor of roads, overseer of the poor, and every four years, a justice of the peace. Township supervisors made up a board of supervisors, which managed county government. At the county level, a sheriff, prosecuting attorney, surveyor of lands, recorder, and assessor were elected for two-year terms. Circuit courts, which took over some of the judicial functions of the county courts, were also established with judges elected for six-year terms.[12]

As originally configured, West Virginia was comprised of forty-four counties. The counties of the eastern panhandle, coveted because they lay along the route of the Baltimore and Ohio Railroad, were allowed the vote on whether to join the new state or not. Occupied by Union troops at the time, six joined the New Dominion; only one county, Frederick, remained with Virginia. This gave West Virginia fifty counties. Five more were created in subsequent decades.[13]

The 1872 convention created the state's current constitution. The new constitution signaled a return to the institutional forms of the 1851 Virginia constitution and to Jacksonian ideals on limited government. The overthrow of the "Yankeefied" township system was a major aspect of this reaction. The constitution replaced the township government with the traditional, Virginia-style, strong county form of local government. County courts composed of at least two justices of the peace and led by a president elected to a four-year term were at the center of the system. County courts were empowered to perform a wide variety of executive and judicial functions. County voters also elected a sheriff for a single term, a surveyor, a prosecuting attorney, one or two assessors, and one or two constables. The county court selected the coroner, overseer of the poor, and surveyor of roads. A sub-unit, the precinct, was created in place of the township. Justices of the peace were elected for four-year terms by the precinct's voters, but it had no other function in county governance. The plural nature of county government, with multiple, elected officials, represented a continuance of the Jacksonian tradition of distrust of unified power and the assurance that the people's voice would be heard, loud and clear, in local policymaking."[14]

Over the years, the 1872 Constitution has been amended sixty-four times. Few have been as important as the 1880 amendment, which completely rewrote Article VII on judicial power. This amendment came on the heels of a U.S. Supreme Court decision which upheld an Iowa case redefining the relationship between state and local governments. Traditionally, local governments had been defined as self-governing, sovereign entities with inherent powers that enabled them to make laws independently of state governments. According to the new ruling, called Dillon's Rule in honor of the Iowa judge who made the initial decision, local governments have no inherent powers. Instead, all local governments derive their powers wholly from the states. As creatures of the state, local governments require specific enabling legislation from state legislatures to authorize whatever functions they perform.[15]

The 1880 constitutional amendment also abandoned the Virginia county court model and put into place the basic structure of county government that is in use today. The general thrust of the amendment was to strengthen the circuit courts at the expense of the county courts. In fact, the framers of this amendment did away with the term county court altogether, substituting the term county commission. The county commissions were left with only some minor judicial functions, settling probate, family law, and election disputes. Justices of the peace were eliminated from the county commission, retaining only a role in handling small claims and misdemeanor cases in their local precincts.

The county commission was delineated as a body with three commissioners, elected to six-year terms. The powers of the county commissions were clearly spelled out and limited:

The county commissions, through their clerks, shall have the custody of all deeds and other papers presented for record in their counties, ... They shall also… have the superintendence and administration of the internal police and fiscal affairs of their counties, including the establishment and regulation of roads, ways, bridges, public landings, ferries and mills, with authority to lay and disburse county levies…[16]

County commissions were also entrusted to conduct elections for county and district officers. The 1880 amendment established them as mere administrative units of the state, a change that continues to have wide impacts today. [17]

Although the state has relieved the counties of some burdens, including most road maintenance and social welfare, it has added a number of responsibilities - to fund public libraries, to construct airports, construct waterworks, to improve streets not in the state road system, to construct and maintain parks, to maintain fire stations, to provide garbage disposal services and operate landfills, to create county planning and zoning commissions, to establish building and housing codes, to construct flood walls, to provide emergency ambulance services, and to fund hospitals and nursing homes.

West Virginia counties face yet another important challenge in the future: preserving their courthouses as architectural monuments in a manner consisted with National Register of Historic Places guidelines. State legislators have been aware of this challenge for over a decade. In 2001, the legislature set up the West Virginia Courthouse Facilities Improvement Authority to help counties preserve their courthouses and improve their facilities. This is an important step in recognizing the value of some of the state's most beautiful buildings. Plato and the Greek philosophers put beauty on the same pedestal as truth and justice as ultimate values. All three values are represented in West Virginia's courthouses. This book provides clear evidence that our courthouses deserve all the TLC that we can muster.

Why Rehabilitate A Courthouse?

Michael Gioulis
Historic Preservation Consultant

As can be seen, most of West Virginia's courthouses are considered historic and were built at least fifty years ago. There is only one courthouse less than five years old and the majority of those less than fifty years old are still at least twenty years old. With this aging building stock, it is no wonder that the counties are scrambling to find funds to maintain, repair and rehabilitate their buildings. It is obvious why counties find it necessary to rehabilitate.

Age

For some, strictly due to the age of the buildings, it is time to repair old finishes, surfaces, structural or other systems. For example, if we are looking at a historic courthouse with an original slate roof, the typical life expectancy of slate varies with the region from which it was quarried; from as little as 75 years to over 175 years. In addition to the slate itself, the more common systems to fail in a slate, or clay tile, roof are the attachment system, and the flashings. Many of the older roofs used a terne coated steel as flashing and a coated nail or galvanized nail for fastening the roof tiles. The base material, sheet steel, requires that the terne coating be painted, and with proper maintenance, it can have a life expectancy of up to ninety years. Sometimes copper was used, and in more recent times, stainless steel. Each of these, unpainted, depending on the gauge or thickness, can last up to 60 or 70 years. Fasteners can have a similar life expectancy. Therefore, the ancillary systems on a historic slate or tile roof generally fail before the slate or tile actually does. Taking all of this into account, on a one hundred year old courthouse with a slate roof, it is likely that the slate is failing, as well as the flashing and gutter system and the attachments. Its replacement therefore is overdue or nearing a critical point.

The same can be said for all systems in a historic building. Plaster may be damaged by moisture or by movement or mechanical abrasion from occupants. Windows may be deteriorating from moisture, rot of the wood elements, weather stripping failures, hardware failure, etc. Flooring may be wearing out. Doors may show hardware failure or deterioration due to age and use. Heating and cooling systems, though many were installed much more recently, have also reached their useful life or may not meet current code requirements. In all, this is a natural evolution of the building and its systems. Anything 100 years old will require some maintenance.

Maintenance

In some buildings, previous maintenance or alterations may have damaged historic materials or compromised historic systems. For example, improper pointing of masonry joints can actually damage the masonry it was intended to protect. Historic mortar was intended to be softer in strength than the masonry it surrounded. Bricks often were more softly fired and of a softer material than modern machine-made bricks. Stone is a natural material and its characteristics may vary depending on where it was quarried, its mineral content, type of stone, how it was laid in the wall, construction and other details. Historic mortar was high in lime content resulting in mortar that was softer than the masonry. As the masonry walls move for structural purposes, or from environmental influences, the mortar would take up this movement, rather than the masonry, which would fail if it were required to move. Many past attempts at masonry restoration used mortar that was available at the time, usually in a higher strength as a result of increase use of cement in lieu of lime content. The result is that when the wall 'breathes" or moves the mortar cannot, so it is the masonry that moves and subsequently cracks.
In other instances, where modern systems have been installed in buildings or there is damage to fabric as a result of the installation of HVAC equipment, wiring, plumbing and other necessary upgrades to the building. Often original or historic fabric was damaged in the installation process.

Repairs

Repairs are often needed for items damaged in the past or for items that have outlived their usefulness.

Rehabilitation

Often, a project is undertaken to meet some need identified in the courthouse, such as new equipment for the clerk, new filing systems, or new court procedures. Often it is a floor plan change due to the differing requirements of modern courthouse use.

Restoration

A project may be undertaken to reverse changes that have occurred in the past. This may be designed to return the courthouse or courtroom or some areas of the building to its original state of grandeur. Three relatively recent projects illustrate this situation: the restoration of the Randolph County Courtroom, Barbour County Courtroom, and Marion County Courtroom. For example, the Barbour County Courtroom had long been covered with modern finishes, and the ceiling lowered with lay-in ceiling tiles hiding its beautiful ornate stained glass dome. The courtroom restoration was begun in 1999, led by Alan D. Moats, Judge of the 19th Judicial Circuit. The modern ceiling was removed, the stained glass and dome was restored, as well as the plaster beams and coffers, resulting in a beautifully preserved original piece of West Virginia's and Barbour County's history.

Upgrades to meet codes

As times change, so do codes and ordinances that protect people and buildings. The Life Safety Code, that which governs fire safety in our edifices, is one example. The Building Code, Americans with Disabilities Act, Heating and Ventilation Codes and others keep up with modern advances in technology and information to protect our citizens. Many code advances are unfortunate results of tragedies, such as many of the fire codes in effect today. For example, as a result of and with the knowledge gained by recent dance club tragedies, our fire codes have been upgraded to reflect a greater determination for the installation of sprinkler systems to protect occupants. Likewise, the ADA has brought a greater awareness of all citizens' desires and requirements for participation in our society and a greater desire to include all persons.

Unfortunately, many of the code requirements can be construed as requiring severe alterations to historic buildings, up to and including the destruction of historic fabric and architectural character. This is not necessarily true. Careful planning and investigation of creative solutions can often result in better protection and less impact to the historic character of the building.

Upgrades to meet programs and changing needs of courthouse functions

Our life is constantly changing, and the way we do business in this modern world is also progressing. Systems and technology not dreamed of in the past are now commonplace. With these changes in our everyday workplace come changes in the buildings that house these activities. For example, computerization and digital storage solutions may make physical deed storage obsolete. Digital research and reference books may make libraries less reliant on large stack space. All of these changes will have an impact on how we use our buildings. Also, increases in public access to our legal system have placed pressure on many courthouses to provide additional courtrooms, judges spaces, magistrates and other needed facilities. Changing technologies also place a burden on the courthouse, often requiring alterations for communications systems and similar elements.

In short, there are many reasons and demands for rehabilitating a courthouse. The natural progression of a society is to update its buildings to change with current needs, and it has been happening to courthouses and public buildings since the beginning of the built environment. It is, however, incumbent upon we who control the changes, decide the rehabilitation, opt for the restoration, to understand and know the best methods to achieve our goals, while simultaneously preserving and protecting those aspects of the courthouse that make it so important to our nation.

The Courthouses

County Reference Map

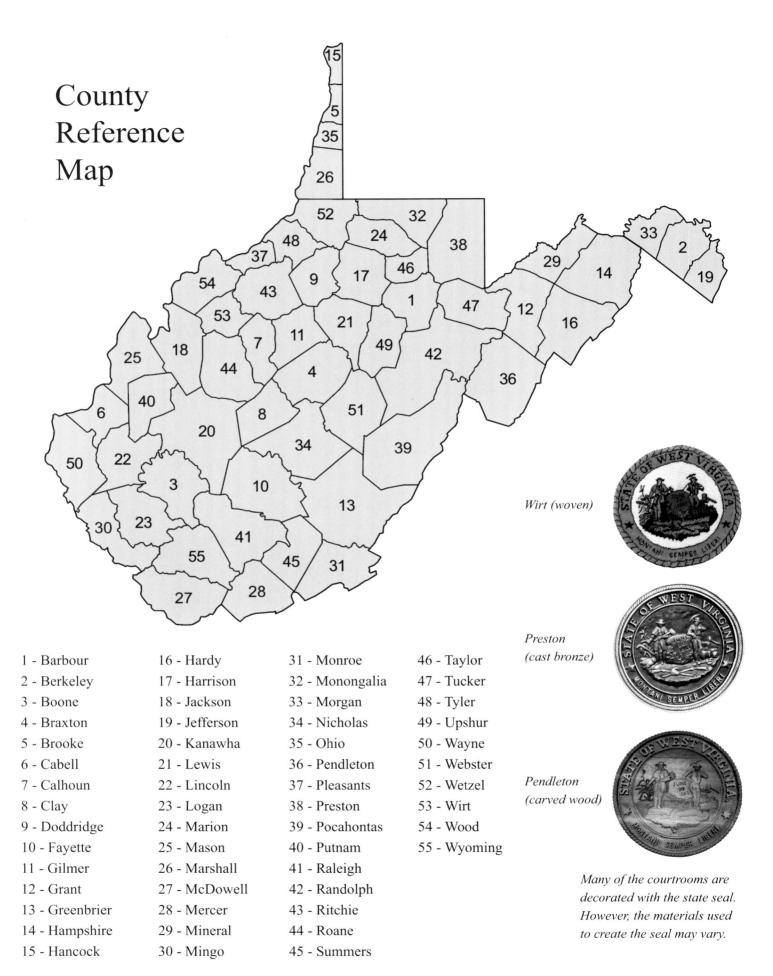

Wirt (woven)

Preston (cast bronze)

Pendleton (carved wood)

Many of the courtrooms are decorated with the state seal. However, the materials used to create the seal may vary.

1 - Barbour	16 - Hardy	31 - Monroe	46 - Taylor
2 - Berkeley	17 - Harrison	32 - Monongalia	47 - Tucker
3 - Boone	18 - Jackson	33 - Morgan	48 - Tyler
4 - Braxton	19 - Jefferson	34 - Nicholas	49 - Upshur
5 - Brooke	20 - Kanawha	35 - Ohio	50 - Wayne
6 - Cabell	21 - Lewis	36 - Pendleton	51 - Webster
7 - Calhoun	22 - Lincoln	37 - Pleasants	52 - Wetzel
8 - Clay	23 - Logan	38 - Preston	53 - Wirt
9 - Doddridge	24 - Marion	39 - Pocahontas	54 - Wood
10 - Fayette	25 - Mason	40 - Putnam	55 - Wyoming
11 - Gilmer	26 - Marshall	41 - Raleigh	
12 - Grant	27 - McDowell	42 - Randolph	
13 - Greenbrier	28 - Mercer	43 - Ritchie	
14 - Hampshire	29 - Mineral	44 - Roane	
15 - Hancock	30 - Mingo	45 - Summers	

Barbour County was created, with Philippi as the county seat, by an act of the Virginia General Assembly on March 3, 1843 from parts of Harrison, Lewis, and Randolph counties. The county, and county seat, were named in honor of Virginia politician and jurist, Philip Pendleton Barbour (1783-1841), who served Virginia in the U.S. House of Representatives, Judge of the United States Circuit Court for the Eastern District of Virginia, and Associate Justice of the U.S. Supreme Court.

A monument to veterans stands on the front, left corner of the courthouse grounds. A WWI doughboy statue tops the memorial.

Barbour County Courthouse
Constructed ~ 1903 / 1905
Style ~ Romanesque Revival
County Seat ~ Philippi

Multiple stained glass panels form the central doorway arch and side panels providing a soft, natural light for the entrance to the courthouse.

The first meeting of the Barbour County court was held on April 3, 1843 at the home of William F. Wilson. The county's justices of the peace elected Lair D. Morrall as county clerk. The next order of business was to nominate a sheriff for referral to the governor. By tradition, the Justice of the Peace that had served the longest became the sheriff. However, it was not clear if Isaac Booth or Joseph McCoy had served the longest as a Justice of the Peace. An election was held, and Joseph McCoy was recommended to the Governor for appointment. The first official courthouse, in a Greek Revival design and modeled after the Hampshire County Courthouse, was completed in 1846. The cost, which included a jail, was $5300.00. With the outbreak of the Civil War, the first flag to fly from the cupola was that of the Confederacy, reflecting the general southern sympathies of the local community. This courthouse served the county until the early 20th century, when the current courthouse was completed.

above: the 1846 courthouse

The architect selected for the courthouse project was J. Charles Fulton (1856-1924). Fulton also served as the architect for the Randolph and Doddridge County courthouses. The courthouse is an excellent example of the Romanesque Revival style perfected by Henry H. Richardson in late 19th century America. The monumental building is constructed of a striated Cleveland Sandstone with brown and pink colorations. While the courthouse was designed to be massive in appearance, it is not without ornamentation.

right: the central tower is an impressive feature. Because of its height, the tower serves as a location for communication antennae.

Carved patterns and column capitols provide detail and display the craftsmanship of the period.

right: the courtroom with suspended ceiling, prior to restoration.

above: a scene in the courtroom of the first courthouse.

right: a view of the restoration work on the exposed skylight and domed ceiling.

As time passed, the courthouse became in need of repair. The stained glass dome had broken and the room suffered water damage. The result was the installation of a suspended ceiling, vinyl flooring and fluorescent lighting.

In 1995, work began to restore the courthouse. The roof was repaired, tiles were replaced, exterior stone work was cleaned, the windows were reconditioned and final exterior work was completed in May 2000 when the bell tower was restored. While exterior work was underway, the interior restoration of the courtroom began in 1999 with the cleaning of the woodwork, the replacement of the wood flooring and restoration of the glass dome.

Once the dropped ceiling was removed, it was evident that the plaster and curved columns were severely damaged. Interior designer and Barbour County native, Genevieve Arbogast, volunteered her services and completed the process of bringing the courtroom as close to the original design as possible. The newly restored courtroom was dedicated on December 19, 2000.

Judge Alan Moats commented,
"... *No great project was ever accomplished without enthusiasm. This project is a testament to what can be accomplished when elected officials, private citizens, the public, and private industry can do in working together for a public cause... This courtroom and courthouse ... is a work of art, it is a masterpiece, and it is worth preserving. It is a treasure that the citizens of the county should be proud of. It is worthy of the citizens of Barbour County and the State of West Virginia.*"

The present courthouse is the county's second, built on the site of the original 1779 courthouse.

This historic structure is located at the corner of King and Queen Streets, in the heart of the downtown. From the city's earliest beginnings, the courthouse was designed to be a mainstay in a public square setting and remains a center piece of Martinsburg.

Berkeley County Courthouse
Constructed ~ 1855 / 1856
Style ~ Neoclassical Revival
County Seat ~ Martinsburg

Berkeley County is the second oldest in the state, created by an act of the House of Burgesses in 1772 from a northern portion of Frederick County, Virginia. It originally included portions of present-day Jefferson and Morgan counties. County records show that the first court was held May 19, 1772 in a house rented from an Edward Beeson. The county seat, then a village of 200 residents, was called Berkeley Court House.

Designed by B&O Railroad Architect, Albert Fink, it is one of the state's oldest courthouses in continuous use. The courthouse design has been though roof modifications in 1880-81, and the addition of a third floor in 1908, that has created the Neoclassical Revival style we see today.

On King Street, the main entrance has a two-story, Ionic column portico capped with a large cornice with decorative entablature. The third floor features are paired pilasters with arched surrounds with a gable pediment and large decorative brackets.

The three-story building has a classic courthouse appearance with a majestic octagonal dome centrally located on the roof. The dome is capped with a spire and weather vane, with smaller domes flanking it.

Modifications of the interior, throughout the years, have been extensive, but elements of its original interior are still evident in the stairways, pressed tin ceilings, and fixtures.

As with many courthouses, the records found within can be quite interesting. *"The History of Berkeley County"* takes note of an excerpt from the will of General Charles Lee, which was recorded, in his own writing, in 1782. *"I desire most earnestly not to be buried in any church or church yard or within a mile of any church or church yard or within a mile of any Presbyterian or Anna Baptist meeting House. For since I have resided in this country, I have kept so much bad company when living that I do not chuse to continue it when dead..."*

Other offices have been moved to the Berkeley County Judicial Center, which was dedicated in October 2006. It was built to consolidate judicial officers located previously in five buildings in the downtown area of Martinsburg. This provided for the ease of use by the public and to enhance security to the judicial officers.

The Judicial Center is an excellent example of adaptive reuse of an historic structure. Originally built in phases from 1917 to 1927, the U-shaped structure was constructed of brick and heavy timber and first served as a woolen mill. After the mill was shut down, it was converted into an outlet mall in the 1980s as a shopping destination for the local community. The outlet mall however did not succeed and the complex again went through another rebirth as a community and technical college prior to becoming the Judicial Center. The 122,606 square foot center houses nine courtrooms and seven hearing rooms for the Circuit, Magistrate, and Family Courts; Clerks of the Circuit and Magistrate Courts; prosecuting attorneys; probation; central holding facility and court support. In April 2010, the Berkeley County Judicial Center received an Honor Award from the West Virginia chapter of the American Institute of Architects (AIA).

Today, the historic courthouse houses all of the functions of the County Clerk's offices with the exception of the Finance and Voter's Registration functions, which are located in an adjacent annex. The courtroom on the second floor often is used for weddings and for functions related to elections.

left: a young couple take their wedding vows in the courtroom.

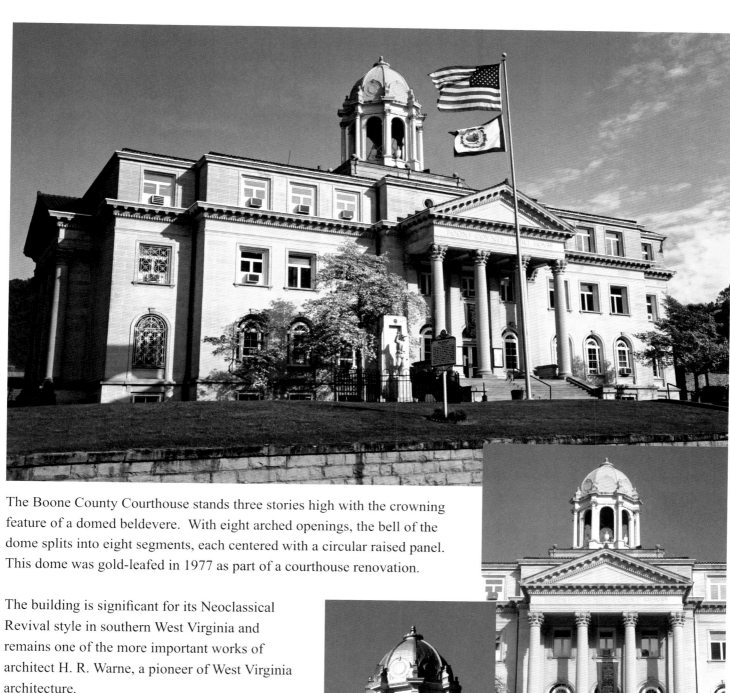

The Boone County Courthouse stands three stories high with the crowning feature of a domed beldevere. With eight arched openings, the bell of the dome splits into eight segments, each centered with a circular raised panel. This dome was gold-leafed in 1977 as part of a courthouse renovation.

The building is significant for its Neoclassical Revival style in southern West Virginia and remains one of the more important works of architect H. R. Warne, a pioneer of West Virginia architecture.

Boone County Courthouse
Constructed ~ 1921 / 1923
Style ~ Neoclassical Revival
County Seat ~ Madison

On March 11, 1847, the Virginia General Assembly created Boone County from Cabell, Logan and Kanawha counties. Named by St. Clair Ballard, a member of the Virginia Assembly, Boone County pays homage to the American folk hero, Daniel Boone. In a speech, Ballard proposed the name of Boone to the greater Assembly and used a harrowing tale in which his mother was rescued by Boone from a group of Native Americans as his method of persuasion.

Boone County's possessed a total of three courthouses through its history, but long before any official government office stood, county officials held court hearings in a log church located at the mouth of Turtle Creek. Later, dedicated court-houses were built. The first one stood until the conflicts of the Civil War swept through the area, and it was burned to the ground. A second courthouse lasted until 1913.

After the second courthouse was deemed unsuited for the county's needs, plans for this courthouse were made, and in 1917 construction began, but problems emerged even after the building's foundation was laid in 1919. Danville, another township present in Boone County, entered as a possible site for the county's seat of government, replacing Madison. This completely halted construction. Madison eventually won the vote, though problems persisted. It was discovered that an Indiana limestone edifice would not be ready for use until 1921.

Other delays and financial issues continued to hinder the project. In 1919 Warne went before the county court and complained that the contractor was not supplying the appropriate materials or enough properly skilled workers to ease the construction along. Finally, the difficulty and controversy was laid to rest when all aspects of the project were placed directly into the hands of the county court.

The courthouse was labeled safe to work in by June, 1921 and was fully completed in 1923.

One of the visual features on the front lawn of the Courthouse is a 7-foot tall bronze statue celebrating the contributions of coal miners to Boone County. The statue was unveiled on Labor Day, 1991.

The second floor of the building is home to the courtroom. A very spacious courtroom features two-level public seating as well as a two balcony areas. However, the balconies are closed and no longer used for seating. Hardwood flooring is used throughout the courtroom.

Polished brass railings accent the litigation well and balconies.

A large skylight of translucent glass, bounded by ceiling beams, allows daylight to add to the overall illumination of the courtroom.

The well appointed Sheriff (left) and Circuit Clerk's offices (right) are examples of recent restoration and renovation efforts in the courthouse.

An interesting feature on the Courthouse square is the memorial dedicated to veterans of the American Revolution.

Located on Main Street within a large courthouse square, this two-story red brick courthouse is the focus of the community's downtown. It is the county's second courthouse. Confederate troops burned the first during the Civil War. A small one-story, wood frame structure served as the court-house during the intervening time.

Braxton County Courthouse
Constructed ~ 1881 / 1882
Style ~ Colonial Revival
County Seat ~ Sutton

When the courtroom was remodeled, some of the panels from the old metal ceiling were saved and used to create furniture for the courtroom.

The interior of the courthouse is, for the most part, in as-built condition. While there have been renovations in the main courtroom on the second floor such as hardwood wainscoting on the wall, the original wood benches for public seating and original judge's bench remain.

Braxton, as with most of West Virginia's counties, was created by an act of the Virginia General Assembly, on January 15, 1836 from sections of Nicholas and Lewis counties. Sutton (as it is known today) was chartered in 1826 when it was part of Nicholas County. It had been known as Newville then later as Suttonville. The town's name was changed to Sutton on March 1, 1837 and incorporated on February 20, 1860.

The first meeting of the County Court of Law and Chancery took place on April 11, 1836 at the home of John D. Sutton. Court records from the first year are well preserved. The following are excerpts from the county records of May 24, 1836: *Benjamin Skidmore, having produced to the Court, William Newlon's receipt (Clerk of Court) for two dollars, the amount imposed by law, leave is granted him for keeping a house of private entertainment in the said County until the first day day of May Court next.* At the same session, the Court proceeded to regulate a variety of charges made by the Sheriff: *for keeping every slave per day, 20 cents; for keeping every horse or mule per day, 8 cents; for all horned cattle or hogs, 4-1/2 cents per day; for keeping sheep or goats, every day 3 cents each.*

All the windows are arched with stone keystones and arched hoods above with stone sills below. The windows on the front elevation are set within a recessed brick bay. The main roof is hip with a gable on the front.

County records show that the original courthouse design concept was authored by Felix J. Baxter, a local resident, and contractors Wood and Atchinson utilized plans and specifications drawn by C.C. Kemble.

Adjacent to the courthouse is the former Braxton County Jail, which sits directly to the northwest on the courthouse lawn. The small two-story, cut sandstone building was built in 1905 and is an interesting historic element to the large downtown square.

The bell that once graced the Courthouse tower, is now on display in the main entry hallway.

The courthouse square is outlined with hand-cut stone walls and large trees; cut stone monuments and other plantings are all enhancements. As is the tradition in many small towns, the courthouse square is often the location for a variety of activities. With the fall season and the arrival of Halloween, the courthouse grounds are decorated with pumpkins and other characters created for the Scarecrow contest as part of the Sutton Fall Festival.

When Brooke County, once part of Ohio County, was established by legislative action of the Commonwealth of Virginia in 1797, Wellsburg (then called Charlestown) became the seat of government, despite its location in the southern-most reaches of the new county.

One of the state's oldest courthouses, it lacks the heavy exterior ornamentation commonly found on late 19th Century public buildings. The flat, Doric portico of the main entrance, the gable roof, and central cupola are the most outstanding exterior features.

Brooke County Courthouse
Constructed ~ 1849
Style ~ Greek Revival
County Seat ~ Wellsburg

The first session of the Brooke County court took place on May 23, 1797 in the home of William Sharpe in Charlestown. At the time the county included what is now Hancock County but Charlestown was the center of population, which resulted in its selection as the seat of county government by balloting of the court.

In June of that year, officials purchased the land where the current courthouse rests from Charles Prather, a man considered to be the town's founding father, and drafted a plan for a courthouse of brick and a jail of stone. A local builder, Samuel Herdman, was hired for the construction, but records indicate the first courthouse was wood, not brick. It opened on April 29, 1799 and remained in use until 1849, when it was razed.

The town was renamed Wellsburg in 1816, in honor of Charles Prather's son-in-law, Alexander Wells, to avoid confusion with two other towns in the state of Virginia that were also called Charlestown. Wells, a successful businessman, is credited as the builder of the first large warehouse in the east.

The County Commissioners, on April 30, 1849, approved the plans to erect a new building for "*a sum not to exceed $6885.*" Documents in the Circuit Clerk's Office list a James Winteringer as the brick sub-contractor. By an action of the County Commission in December of that year, he was awarded a sum of $80.83 above his original contract "*for extra work to cover a mistake made by one of the commissioners as to the quality of the brick [and] also the sum of $4.24 for water to dampen the bricks when building ...*" During construction, the Brooke Academy housed county offices and courts.

Brook County Court-House and Jail, Wellsburg, W. Va.

Many upgrades, repairs, and remodels have been made since 1849: an addition in 1913, underpinning of the foundation in 1933, a WPA repair of flood damage in 1936, and a new brick veneer in 1941. The interior, including the courtroom, has been modernized in design. The most recent addition, the annex on the south side of the structure was added in the 1970s.

The county has maintained its records and local documents reveal that during the first year of the courts, the Grand Jury reported bills of indictment against the following persons: *James Davidson for retailing Whiskey at 10c per half pint; Alexander Wells for profane swearing..83c and cost; Richard Speer for profane swearing..83c and costs. During the first session of court, the following rates were to be observed by the Ordinary (Hotel) keeper: Breakfast and Supper - 20 c; Dinner - 25 c; Lodging - 5c; Hay, per night - 17c; Oats or grain, per Quart - 2c; Whiskey, 1/2 pint - 9c; Common Rum, 1/2 pint - 18c; French Brandy, 1/2 pint -30c; Maderia Wine, Per Quart - 1.75; Sherry Wine, Per Quart - 1.20; and Beer - 9c.*

In the June term of Court, 1800, records show a sale of a slave, Dinah, 19 years old, sold by Sam Wheeler, to Richard Wells, for $265.76. The 1802 records also show that during the term of the County Court, Ann Blair (Mrs. James Blair), accused of witchcraft by Calop and Rachel Pumphry, was declared innocent by the court.

The courthouse is part of the town square and sits next to the Wellsburg City Building, that was constructed in 1940. This site was first used for a market house that was built in 1828 and survived until 1892. It was replaced by the first City Hall in 1893, that was later destroyed by fire in 1939.

The Cabell County Courthouse is not only the seat of county government, but represents the growth and evolution of the city of Huntington as a major urban transportation and industrial center. The grand, Beaux Arts Classical courthouse has a prominent place is the community, dominating the park-like court square.

The main entrance is several steps above ground level and leads from the large, well-landscaped grounds which is part of the Beaux Arts design.

A view of the backside of the courthouse and expansive, wooded grounds that surround the building.

Cabell County Courthouse
Constructed ~ 1899 / 1901
Style ~ Beaux Arts
County Seat ~ Huntington

Created by an act of the General Assembly of Virginia in 1809, the county was named for Virginia Governor William H. Cabell (1805-08). It was derived from Kanawha County and included all of present-day Lincoln, Mingo and Wayne counties and part of each of the counties of Boone, Logan, and Putnam.

Court session was first held in 1809 at the home of William Merritt, near Barboursville and the first official courthouse was commissioned to be built near Guyandotte in 1812. By 1814, Barboursville was established as the permanent county seat. The only interruption in county government was a nearly two year period during the Civil War when the town was taken over by the Confederacy and records moved to Guyandotte for safe keeping. The final move of the county seat came in 1887, when Huntington was selected by voters to be the new center of government. The vote reflected the city's development as the transportation center of the region and terminus for Collis P. Huntington's C&O Railroad.

Property for the courthouse square was purchased in 1892, the foundation laid in 1896, and construction began in the summer of 1899. The extended time was due to a halt in construction with the Panic of 1983. The courthouse was completed on December 4, 1901 at an approximate cost of $100,000.00.

The original courthouse is the center of the present-day building; a square plan with short wings extending to the east and west and a standing seam copper dome and seven-story clock tower capping the structure. The first story and raised basement facade is rusticated (rough) Berea sandstone, above which is smooth coursed ashlar (the masonry lies within the same course or row). The differences in the stone give weight to a building, indicating its importance.

The courthouse is grand is scale with an impressive front facade that is five bays wide and designed to create a second-story balcony. The bays are topped by a central arched window. Typical to the Beaux Arts design, there are elaborate elements, including cartouches, that can be found above the first story windows

39

The interior of the courthouse has retained original features that are equal to the exterior. The main element is the two-story rotunda with a spiraling stair and interior dome. The dome, with a central oculus (window), is plastered and divided into twelve segments by ornamentation in a rope motif.

When looking from the second story balcony, which has an ornamental iron balustrade, you can easily see tile design of the terrazo floor. A pattern with a border of terrazo and mosaic tile extends down the hallways of the first floor.

left: the second floor balustrade.

below: a view from the second floor balcony.

below: beneath the dome and continuing around the wall is a detailed decorative trim that complements the patterns in the dome.

As Huntington and the county continued to grow in the 20th century, two architecturally compatible wings were added to meet the increased needs of county government. The west-wing was completed in 1924 and the east-wing in 1940. The primary circuit courtroom is in the west addition and has been extensively remodeled. Two additional circuit courtrooms are in the east wing and are also modern in design.

The current Art Moderne designed courthouse was constructed between 1940 and 1942 by the Works Progress Administration (WPA) at a cost of $170,000. Consistent with the style, the two-story building is flat roofed, with a square entrance tower, and is three-stories in height.

The courthouse is constructed of cutstone. To add interest, the body of the building has random course ashlar stone with smooth stone accents. It gives an impression of an ancient temple - an important social or governmental center.

Calhoun County Courthouse
Constructed ~ 1940 / 1942
Style ~ Art Moderne
County Seat ~ Grantsville

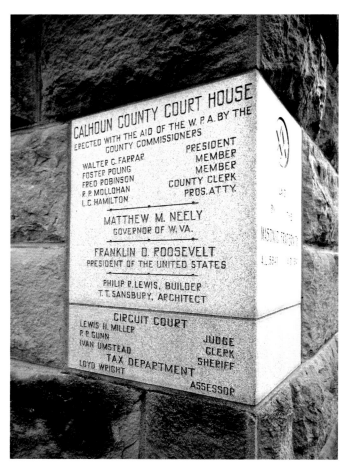

Calhoun County was created March 5, 1856 from a section of Gilmer County by an act of the Virginia General Assembly, and the first court was held within a month. The county was named after John Caldwell Calhoun, a South Carolina legislator and cabinet member for President James Monroe.

Grantsville, the current county seat, was not always the center of Calhoun county government. In the fall of 1856, the justices of the county court met at a home in Arnoldsburg. The act creating the county specified that the county's residents were to determine the permanent county seat. Voters chose Pine Bottom, at the mouth of Yellow Creek, as the first county general election in November 1856. However, the county justices did not all agree, and two county courts emerged, one in Arnoldsburg, and the other in Pine Bottom. Differences were briefly resolved and a unified county court was established at Yellow Creek, the current site of Brooksville, in September, 1857. The following year, the county seat was again moved back to Arnoldsburg and the county court acquired land to build a courthouse.

The cornerstone, laid by members of the local Masonic order, identify county officials and, notably, that the President at the time of construction was Franklin D. Roosevelt.

In 1862, Union forces captured Arnoldsburg and the state legislature then moved the county seat to Grantsville. At the conclusion of the Civil War, the citizens of Arnoldsburg demanded that the county seat be returned. A fire of mysterious origin destroyed the Granstville courthouse, which was still under construction, in 1869. The county court continued to move until an election to settle the matter was held in October that same year, when the county electorate selected Grantsville as the permanent county seat and a courthouse was constructed.

The citizens of Arnoldsburg continued to protest until 1898, when a vote of 935-925 determined that the county seat would be permanently established in Grantsville. Two years later, the county government replaced the courthouse with a brick building at a cost of $8,400. It was, in turn, replaced in 1941 with the courthouse in use today.

This view shows the full courthouse and the Sheriff's office / old jail to the rear of the building.

Interestingly, counsel for the defense and prosecution share the same table in the courtroom.

While the courthouse appears quite small from the exterior, when you enter the main lobby it is very large. The staircases, which are concrete with pipe railing, lead to the main courtroom as well as to access to the exterior balcony.

The courtroom is mostly original, but the ceiling has been lowered and is covered with suspended ceiling panels and stucco. When the ceiling was lowered, it covered the original balcony area. The spectator area has oak benches and is separated from the judge's bench by an oak railing. The courtroom has numerous windows which gives the room abundant natural light and creates a more spacious feel.

above: the signs for the county offices were hand-lettered on each door by the Circuit Clerk, giving the courthouse a personal touch.

A jail, which was constructed in the style of a residence, sits directly behind the courthouse. Due to its architectural style and the materials used in its construction, the jail was probably built within the same time period as the courthouse and by the WPA.

While the courthouse lawn is not large, a beautiful granite monument, dedicated to all Calhoun County veterans, stands at the southwest corner.

Completed in 1978, the modern red brick courthouse was constructed at a cost of $1.3 million. In the program from the dedication ceremony, the sentiments of the community were evident regarding the new government building: "*it stands as a monument to the men and women of Clay County, both public servants and private citizens, who helped in its creation. Generations of Clay Countians will benefit from it.*"

Columns and arches form the entry colonnade - the stylistic elements are a reminder of classic courthouse design.

Clay County Courthouse
Constructed ~ 1978
Style ~ Modern / Contemporary
County Seat ~ Clay

Clay County, named the Kentucky Senator, Henry Clay, was formed in 1858 from parts of Braxton, Kanawha and Nicholas counties. The act creating the county declared that the county seat be located near the mouth of Buffalo Creek, in the area known as Marshall. The first county court was held at a private home on July 12, 1858. The order of business for the new county court was the setting the of dates for electing the county government's officials and future court meetings. The first Circuit Court convened October 21, 1858 and the first public elections were held in May, 1859. At that time, there were 293 registered voters in the county.

An act of the Legislature, passed October 10, 1863, officially changed the name of the town from Marshall to Henry, honoring Henry Clay. The local citizens generally referred to the county seat as Clay Court House, because the courthouse was a center of the town's social and economic activities. This was such common place that it was recognized by the US Postal Service. In 1927, the town's name was finally changed to Clay.

Clay County has one of the few modern design courthouses in the state. The exterior archways and smooth surfaces have replaced the ornamentation found in the design of the courthouses from previous generations.

While contemporary in style, the courthouse continues the tradition of creating a space to honor those who have served their country. A memorial park for war veterans in on the courthouse grounds. The memorial consists of three marble monuments: one to Korean veterans; one to Vietnam veterans; and the tallest of the three, the monument to the veterans of World War I and II.

The interior, contemporary style was created to provide greater working space for the county employees and accommodate the needs of citizens. This was done in a pleasing and practical fashion as seen in the well-lit first floor atrium and open stairwells.

The modern courtroom features a combination of carved wood and textured brass panels, creating a warm and welcoming atmosphere.

The current courthouse is the third in the county, the first being a log structure that was commissioned by the County Court in 1858 and completed following the Civil War in 1865. The county's second courthouse, a Neoclassical Revival, two-story building still stands in the community. It sits upon a terraced hill directly overlooking Main Street at the same location of the original log courthouse. It was constructed in 1902 and designed by Frank L. Packard, whose firm, Packard and Yost, designed the Marion County Courthouse. Referred to as the Historic Clay County Courthouse, it is still utilized by the county to house the Magistrate's offices. The large courtroom is used as a museum repository for the Clay County Historical Society. The building was listed individually on the National Register of Historic Places in 1979.

Dominating the landscape in West Union, the Doddridge County Courthouse is a striking image.
The two and one-half story building, with an asymmetrical design, rich red brick and stone details,
reflects the art of the stone mason and the architectural trends of the late Victorian era.

Doddridge County Courthouse
Constructed ~ 1899 / 1903
Style ~ Romanesque Revival
County Seat ~ West Union

Doddridge County was founded in 1845 from parts of Harrison, Tyler, Ritchie and Lewis counties. It was named for Philip Doddridge (1772-1832), a lawyer, orator, and spokesman of western Virginia. The county court first met at the home of Nathan Davis, a prominent West Union land owner, in the year of the county's founding. Davis gave his house and land to the county, establishing the location of the courthouses. West Union is the largest community within the county and has benefited from the Northwestern Turnpike, the B&O Railroad and U.S. Route 50.

Replacing a courthouse that was destroyed by fire, the present courthouse is known for the its strong vertical elements, steeply pitched gables and prominent towers. The well preserved pressed red brick facades are accented with brick coursing and with vertical and horizontal limestone banding.

Finished stone and quoin work accentuate arches in the structure while foliate-style carvings, which were popular at the time of construction, embellish the space above the massive arched entrance. The stone masonry for the courthouse is well represented in the arch, which is comprised of large radiating segments of limestone. Fanciful visages look down on those who enter the courthouse.

Before entering the courthouse, a look upward to the center of the front-facing gable, will reveal a stone pedestal carrying a classical-style figure representing "Justice" standing above a balconied window.

Flanking the main entrance is the massive clock tower. The original 1903 E. Howard Clock Company clock of Boston, was replaced in 1973 with one from the I.T. Verdon Company of Cincinnati. The only major alteration to the building was the removal of the tower's spire, due to structural deterioration, in 1969.

Another well-known feature of the exterior is the rounded bay at the north corner of the building. It has a conical roof, and each window, from the raised basement to the attic, is stained glass.

The interior of the courthouse has remained much the same as when it was built. The major corridors and rooms, original woodwork, original iron railings in the stairwells and stained glass features are in excellent condition.

The second floor courtroom is a large, octagonal space with classic-style lighting fixtures and original detailing. A large mural with a figure of "Justice" holding the scales dominates the wall behind the dais and judge's bench. The cast iron and wood seating, is turn-of-the-century. High, recessed openings in the front and sides of the courtroom contribute to the spacious, open environment.

49

The Romanesque Revival courthouse sits within an expansive space on Court Street. The two and one-half story courthouse is known for its stone porches and columns with Romanesque capitols. A broad, stone walkway services the main entry of the courthouse.

Fayette County Courthouse
Constructed ~ 1895
Style ~ Romanesque Revival
County Seat ~ Fayetteville

Fayetteville, originally know as Vandalia for settler Abraham Vandal, was selected as the county seat in 1837. In 1838 and 1839, levies in the amount of $1500.00 funded the construction of the first courthouse, which was in use until 1861, when it was destroyed by Union troops. Following the Civil War, the second courthouse was built, but then replaced in 1889. The third building survived until a fire struck in 1893. The fourth, and current courthouse, was completed in 1895 at cost of $58,297.25. Part of its cost was defrayed by utilizing materials from the courthouse which had burned.

Fayette County was created by an act of the Virginia General Assembly in 1831 from parts of Greenbrier, Kanawha, Logan and Nicholas counties. At the time of its formation, it contained land which would eventually be included in the boundaries of Raleigh and Summers counties. The county and town were named in honor of the Marquis de LaFayette, a French aristocrat and Major-General under General George Washington during the American Revolutionary War. A life-size bronze statue of LaFayette, commissioned by the Fayette County Historic Landmarks Commission, was erected on the courthouse lawn in 2004.

The exterior of the courthouse is quite decorative. The porches have balustraded balconies of stone, and the basement and first floor windows have stone lintels, while the windows of the second story are arched and have arched transoms with arched stone lintels. The most outstanding features are the animal and human carvings in many of the pilaster capitals on the corner chimneys and dormers and in a circular design in the gable of the central dormer.

The interior has retained the central and secondary cast iron stairs, tile floors, and some of the wood paneled doors and wainscoting. The second-floor courtroom, which occupies the main space of the second story, is entered though a handsome, oak door with fanlight transom.

One of the hallmarks of the courthouse is the extensive use of well maintained wood trim throughout the building.

A large number of exterior windows provide ample natural light, giving a general warm glow to to the interior spaces.

The Gilmer County Courthouse sits atop a hill overlooking the county seat of Glenville. The Neoclassical Revival courthouse is surrounded by a grassy lawn, and entered via a long stone walkaway. Tripartite round lights with black, iron bases on stone pedestals help create a grand entrance to this seat of county government.

A granite, war memorial, located on the lawn in front of the building, completes the exterior.

Gilmer County Courthouse
Constructed ~ 1922 / 1924
Style ~ Neoclassical Revival
County Seat ~ Glenville

Gilmer County was formed by an Act of the Virginia Assembly, February 3, 1845 from parts of Kanawha and Lewis counties. Named for Thomas W. Gilmer, 28th Governor of Virginia, the organization of the county's government, but not the designation of county seat, began in DeKalb.

Glenville, which at that time was know as "The Ford" for its location where the old state road from Weston to Charleston crossed the Little Kanawha River, was also a desirable location for the county seat. A disagreement over which community, DeKalb or Glenville, would serve as the county seat, created great activity.

A vote was held to determine the center of government, with the majority of 66 votes cast for Glenville, and "the crier was ordered to make the proclamation of the result from the courthouse door." Officials decided to complete the first court term that was in session in DeKalb, until an official courthouse could be built in Glenville. At the June session, there was not total agreement on the move. Those in favor met in Glenville for the session, but the clerk refused to bring records from DeKalb. The Glenville court members took action to acquire the county seat. They road on horseback to DeKalb and arrived before the adjournment of court. Their numbers, added to those already in DeKalb that favored the move, provided the majority vote to adjourn to Glenville. (Glenville Historical Society, 1994)

There would be one more move back to DeKalb in 1846 due to a legal dispute over the land for the courthouse, but after 2 months, Glenville was permanently established as the county seat. The first courthouse was completed c.1850; the second in 1872; and the current courthouse in 1923.

Built at a cost of $99,000, the courthouse is a two-story, brick and stone building with limestone detailing and a sandstone foundation. Doric columns support the gabled portico that has a center round louver (oculus). Three bay recessed wings flank the portico and contain windows with brick hoods, with keystones and smooth stone sills.

The interior of the courthouse has undergone some modernization for individual offices, but the original plan is still evident. The courtroom is original in size, layout, and has retained the oak woodwork. The judge's bench is oak with paneling and it is flanked by tall narrow windows with a clerestory window above. A spindled oak rail separates the judge's area from the spectators, who are provided theater-style wood seats with cast iron framing.

In the lobby, the floor is mosaic tile and the staircases have metal railings, newel posts and panels.

Glenville State College lies directly northeast of the courthouse and a two-story, brick annex, constructed in 1974, is located to the rear of the courthouse. The annex provides the needed space for county administration while allowing the historic courthouse to retain much of its original configuration.

Grant County, named in honor of General Ulysses S. Grant, was formed following the Civil War on February 14, 1866 from a portion of Hardy County. Local history attributes strong Union sentiments as a reason for the drawing of the county lines, as Hardy County had a number of Confederate supporters.

above: the Grant County Courthouse Annex

Grant County Courthouse

Constructed ~ 1976
Style ~ Modern / Contemporary
County Seat ~ Petersburg

56

After several locations, Petersburg was selected as the county seat by a vote of the citizenry. County records show that the area was settled in 1745, the first post office was opened in 1833, and the town incorporated in the Commonwealth of Virginia in 1845. The town has gone by the names of Lunice Creek and Grant Court House. Petersburg was incorporated by the West Virginia legislature in 1910.

In 1976, the present courthouse, of Modern/Contemporary design, was completed. The courthouse reflects the architectural and construction trends of the time, with the philosophy that "form follows function" and that buildings were to focus on simplicity and with the elimination of unnecessary detail. The style represented the concept that the natural appearance of a material should be seen rather than concealed. This was also the time that builders used more industrially-produced materials.

Grant County is one of three counties, the others being Preston and Tucker, that converge at the Fairfax Stone. This point marked the western boundary of more than 5 million acres of land inherited by Lord Thomas Fairfax, from a land grant to his family by King Charles II of England. A document signed by Fairfax in 1752, is framed and on display in the courthouse. While faded with time and difficult to read, it appears to be related to a land dispute within the present-day county.

right: a segment of a land grant map from the Library of Congress showing part of the lands owned by Lord Fairfax in 1737, in what was then northern Virginia.

The historic, Neoclassical Revival courthouse, which preceded the current courthouse, is no longer is use but still stands within the community. The original portion of this building was constructed in 1879 and remodeled in 1909.

The courtroom is contemporary in design with modern, recessed lighting, which is pooled over the litigation well. A carved, wooden, state seal dominates the wall behind the judges bench.

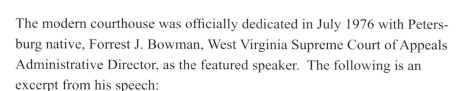

The modern courthouse was officially dedicated in July 1976 with Petersburg native, Forrest J. Bowman, West Virginia Supreme Court of Appeals Administrative Director, as the featured speaker. The following is an excerpt from his speech:

"It is particularly fitting that we should dedicate this courthouse on the eve of the 200th birthday of our nation's independence, for this building, more than any other, represents what our country is about. Watch the common people of this county as they pay their taxes, cast their ballots and go about the ordinary business of dealing with their government in this Courthouse. That is the real drama of life. We are present at the beginning of America's third century and we need not simply give hints as to a better order of things. We can actually be a part of it here in this courthouse."

As part of the ceremony, an American flag, presented by the Veterans of Foreign Wars Post 6454 to the County Commission, was raised while the Petersburg High School Viking Band played the National Anthem. The community's Rotary Club presented a time capsule to the citizens of the county that contained the by-laws of Petersburg, an American Flag, a West Virginia Blue Book, letters from local, state and national politicians, a set of Bicentennial coins, letters from county residents to future relatives, the July 4th edition of the Grant County Press, a copy of Forrest J. Bowman's dedication speech, and pictures of the new Courthouses. The capsule is to be opened in 2076.

The time capsule is located in the walkway in front of the main entrance.

Greenbrier County was created by an act of the Virginia General Assembly in October 1777 from parts of Montgomery and Botetourt counties. Named in honor of the principal river that flows through the county, it is considered the mother county of southern West Virginia. Eleven counties were created, either in whole or in part, from its original territory: Boone, Cabell, Jackson, Kanawha, Mason, Monroe, Nicholas, Putnam, Roane, Wayne, and Webster.

Greenbrier County Courthouse

Constructed ~ 1837
Style ~ Greek Revival
County Seat ~ Lewisburg

Lewisburg, the county seat, was originally called The Savannah, Fort Savannah, and Camp Union, before eventually being named for General Andrew Lewis, who served in both the French and Indian and American Revolutionary Wars. The town's name was officially recognized as Lewisburg when it was incorporated by the Virginia General Assembly in 1782.

A stone obelisk on the courthouse lawn holds bronze tablets that bear witness to the history of Greenbrier County.

The first court session in the county was March, 1780, in the home of John Stuart. In March 1785, a courthouse was ordered to be constructed, but delays occurred, in part due to a heated debate with the residents who would eventually be part of Monroe County. Residents complained that a courthouse in Lewisburg was too great a distance and the Greenbrier River created a barrier between the two regions. The courthouse construction did move forward following the establishment of Monroe County in 1799.

above: the home of John Stuart and site of the first county court meeting.

A bronze plaque commemorates the contribution of John Stuart to the county.

In March of 1800, Michael Bower provided a lot to the town with the stipulation it be used as the site for the courthouse. A three-story, stone courthouse served as the center of county government for 35 years. The current courthouse, which is the oldest functioning courthouse in West Virginia, was erected in 1837 in the Greek Revival style. The construction of this courthouse was mandated by the Virginia General Assembly, as Lewisburg was to be the annual seat for the Commonwealth's Supreme Court of Appeals for those living west of the Appalachians. The courthouse would be one of the first buildings for such purposes west of the mountains.

The classic cupola sits atop the original courthouse and still houses a traditional bell.

above: the annex wing of the courthouse. A new addition is planned at the time of this publication.

The building was constructed of locally fired brick by brickmason, John W. Dunn, a master builder of the region at that time. It is two stories in the front, and three in the rear due to the significant slope of the building lot. The Tuscan columns at the front entrance are brick with a smooth plaster finish and support a pediment entrance portico. A cupola belfry adorns the original part of the building. The flanking wings were added in 1937 and 1963 to accommodate a growing community and increasing needs of the citizenry. The interior of the courthouse has been altered over time and very few original elements are visible.

There are many colorful events that are part of a courthouse history and the Greenbrier County Courthouse is considered to be the location in which testimony from a ghost helped to convict a murderer. Zona Heaster Shue, 1876–1897, is known as the Greenbrier Ghost. Local history recorded that she died mysteriously shortly after her marriage. It was assumed that she died of natural causes until her "spirit" appeared in a dream to her mother, and accused her husband, Edward Shue, of murder. The mother, Mary Heaster, said that her daughter appeared to tell her how the husband, a blacksmith, broke her neck in a fit of rage. The body was exhumed and an examination supported Mary Heaster's account. Edward Shue was found guilty of murder and sentenced to the state prison at Moundsville, Marshall County.

The courtroom is arranged in a classic style. Well maintained bench seating is provided for spectators. The wall behind the judge's bench is highlighted by three, well appointed windows. There are two circuit courtrooms.

The two-story, brick and sandstone building features a large, south-facing portico that is supported by four Ionic columns. Decorative trim and molding accent the area above the portico and add to the impressive entrance. Fanlight windows are above the double-doors of the main entrance and balcony. The balcony has a decorative wrought iron railing.

Hampshire County Courthouse
Constructed ~ 1921 / 1922
Style ~ Neoclassical Revival
County Seat ~ Romney

A large cupola with cardinal directions dominates the Neoclassical Revival courthouse.

Hampshire County was formed in 1754 from parts of Frederick and Augusta counties, Virginia. The county seat, originally referred to as Pearsall's Settlement, was dedicated as the county seat in 1762, and renamed Romney by Lord Fairfax to commemorate an English seaport. That same year, a survey party was sent by Fairfax to layout the town. An early task was the construction of a wooden courthouse in the court square which stood until 1833 when a second courthouse was built. By 1920, the county required a larger courthouse and this began the process for the building we see today.

The courthouse interior is well maintained and features a long, wide hallway, with offices located on either side. The second floor houses the courtroom, judge's chambers, and jury room. The courtroom is quite large with a domed ceiling encircled by squared, rose medallions, each of which holds an electric light.

The large spectator gallery is a reminder that court days were important sources of entertainment in rural, southern regions, and the courtroom was expected to seat all those who traveled to witness the trials.

A walnut panel with an eagle and shield provides the backdrop for the judge's bench.

63

To the rear of the courthouse, is a two-story, cut-stone, annex. Built circa 1934, the annex houses offices of public officials and county government.

Located one block from the courthouse is the Hampshire County Judicial Center, which was completed in 2008. This two-story complex houses the county's circuit, magistrates and family courts as well as other judicial-related offices.

A memorial statue, honoring the World War I soldiers of Hampshire County, stands in front of the building. Erected in 1928 and created by the Romney Marble and Granite Works, it was a gift to the people of Hampshire County from The Hampshire Review. Governor J. J. Cornwell, a former editor of the newspaper, dedicated the monument.

A bronze plaque on the base carries this message with a list of the twenty-seven local soldiers who died in the war :

IN HONOR OF HAMPSHIRE'S SONS WHO GAVE THEIR LIVES AND THEIR SERVICE IN THE WORLD WAR "WE ARE THE DEAD, SHORT DAYS AGO WE LIVED, FELT DAWN, SAW SUNSET GLOW, LOVED AND WERE LOVED."

Romney is known for its Civil War history. While no battles where fought in the town, it changed hands fifty-six times before the war ended. This exchange caused Governor Boreman, in 1865, to order the the circuit court of Hampshire County, along with all of county records, property books, and papers, to be removed to the town of Piedmont. He eventually issued the order for the return to Romney.

A short distance from the courthouse is the Indian Mound Cemetery. It is the site of what is considered the first official Confederate memorial, which was dedicated in 1867. The inscription reads, "*The Daughters of Old Hampshire erect this tribute of affection to her heroic sons who fell in defence of Southern Rights.*" To be fair, the sacrifices of both sides in the Civil War are honored in the community.

The courthouse presents an elegant, yet simple design in a compact form.

As the scope and functions of local government grew in the 20th Century, county government needed more office space. As a result, an addition to the south side of the courthouse was added in 1968, which now houses the Sheriff's Office.

Hancock County Courthouse
Constructed ~ 1921
Style ~ Neoclassical Revival
County Seat ~ New Cumberland

Delegate Thomas Bambrick of New Manchester, Brooke County, representing the citizens of the most northern part of his district and the state, convinced the legislature of the Commonwealth of Virginia to separate the county north of the village of Hollidays Cove and to create Hancock County. That legislation of January 15, 1848 created what would become the smallest political entity of the State of West Virginia when it entered the Union on June 20, 1863.

The enabling law contained a provision which proved troublesome: where to locate the courthouse. It called for "the permanent place for holding several courts [to be] at the Town of New Manchester, unless otherwise decided by the vote of the majority of the lawful voters." At the new county's first election, a separate ballot contained two columns: "For New Manchester" and "For New Cumberland." Voters chose New Cumberland by a margin of 13 votes, but court officials who had already conducted their initial sessions at the home of Samuel Allison in New Manchester in April, 1848 refused to move.

above: the New Cumberland courthouse in 1902 from a postcard of the period.

In 1849, the county erected its first courthouse, a "severely plain" two story brick structure with a keystone arch, a fanlight transom, and a belfry. Its first session came on February 11, 1850. Except for a brief period when the county seat moved to New Cumberland, after a second county-wide vote, the New Manchester building served Hancock County citizens until 1884. Thereafter, it fell into disrepair. Nevertheless, it earned a place on the National Register of Historic Places in 1973, only to be razed in the summer of 1985.

The game of judicial musical chairs seemingly ended in 1884, when the court and county offices moved to New Cumberland, but, in 1905, residents of Chester tried and almost succeeded in getting the seat of government moved to their city. New Cumberland remained the governmental center by a margin of only nine votes, 926 to 917. Since the courthouse removed to New Cumberland, three different buildings have occupied the lot on Court Street. The first was razed in 1905 and replaced by a courthouse which burned on March 20, 1920.

After voter approval of $100,000 in bonds, the current courthouse was built and opened for judicial and bureaucratic business on November 17, 1921.

While compact in size, the courtroom is inviting and very functional in layout. The seating and bench area are offset, providing a wide, side isle for ease of access.

The current structure is modest in size and design: a plain grey façade with a transom fanlight, Greek-inspired pediment, and two pairs of Corinthian columns.

Every county can tell of unusual trials, and Hancock County had one such trial is 1969 when Frank Daminger, a resident of Newell, sued 10 of his neighbors for slander after they allegedly called him "a warlock" and accused him of practicing witchcraft.

In the lawsuit filing, Daminger conceded that he had *"studied witchcraft for the past 15 years."* The trial, which lasted only 2 days and ended in a dismissal, appeared to have been a case of gossip that went beyond neighbors chatting over the backyard fence. Nonetheless, potential jurors where asked if they believed in witchcraft, and during the first day of the trial, the entire court went to the cemetery where neighbors alleged that Daminger held a "Black Mass." When asked by a reporter if he would continue to study witchcraft. Daminger replied, *"Certainly, but it is purely academic study, combined with curiosity."*

The west-facing courthouse, overlooking the town, has no landscaped grounds, but there is a Civil War monument dedicated *"To The Perpetual Memory Of The Defenders Of The Union 1861-1865."* Dedicated on May 30, 1886, it honors the Hancock County soldiers who served in battles at Piedmont, Cedar Creek, Winchester, and Appomattox. After a restoration in 1994, a rededication was held on April 28, 1995.

The present three-story, red brick courthouse was constructed from 1911 to 1913 in the Neoclassical Revival style. This is the fourth courthouse for the county. Hardy is the only county in the state with three courthouses still standing.

The courthouse is set back from the street on a large lot. A wide walk provides access to the entry. A low wall marks the edge of the courthouse grounds.

Hardy County Courthouse
Constructed ~ 1911 / 1913
Style ~ Neoclassical Revival
County Seat ~ Moorefield

The courthouse is impressive with gable porticos on two sides, supported by three-story tall stone Ionic columns. The porticos and the large projecting cornice with ornamental brackets dominate the facade. The entrance door is flanked by paneled and glazed sidelights.

The original windows above the entrance portico were two stories tall, from the second floor up to the third, but these have been replaced with shorter, modern windows.

Hardy County was formed from a portion of Hampshire County in 1785 and named for a Virginia attorney and Congressman, Samuel Hardy. Moorefield was selected as the county seat in 1786 and named for Conrad Moore upon whose land the town was sited. While Moorefield did not become the county seat until 1786, it was first chartered by the Virginia General Assembly in 1777.

The first Court house was built in 1786 of logs and was described as a two-story structure 26 feet by 20 feet. It, and a log jail were located on Moorefield Town lots 34 and 35 on the southeast corner of Winchester Avenue and Franklin Street, now called Elm Street. These two lots were reserved for public use when the Moorefield Town Lots were laid out in 1777. During the Civil War, on May 2, 1864, the county court met at the home of John Mathias. The reason for the move from the court house was given as the proximity of the enemy. This log house, built in the late 1700s, can be seen along State Route 259 in Mathias and has had extensive work to preserve it. While not an official court house, it was the home of the court for at least one day.

above: an old photo of the third courthouse

When it came time to build the second court house the old log structure was moved to make room for the new. Over the years the old courthouse was moved to various lots and housed several businesses on Main and Washington Streets. It eventually became part of a house that has since been town down.

The second courthouse, built of brick in the federal style of architecture in 1794 and added to in 1833, still stands at the corner of Winchester Avenue and Elm Street. It was the courthouse until 1860. After that time the building was used for a private residence, a girl's school, law office, assessor office and print shop. The Hardy County Democrat newspaper was published there 1897-1902. The building is now an apartment house.

The third court house built of brick in the gothic style of architecture was finished in 1860 and was located on Main Street. It too still stands and is across Main St. from the Presbyterian Church. Today it bears no resemblance to the original structure. The courtyard in front of the court house was filled in with store fronts that have housed numerous retail shops and a pool hall. The main part of the building was converted to apartments and is still used for that purpose.

Following in a tradition set in previous courthouses the building was and is occasionally used for non-official business. In 1920, the Methodist Church was to be torn down to build a new and bigger one on the same lot. The members petitioned the county to hold services in the courtroom. The request was granted and the congregation held services there from February 8, 1920, until March 12, 1922.

The block occupied by the courthouse is a well maintained pastoral landscape.

The courtroom is laid out in a classic arrangement dominated by the warm tones of the wood trim.

A veterans memorial sits at the corner of the courthouse lawn.

Thanks to Eleanor L. Heishman for Hardy County historical information.

The Art Moderne courthouse is the fourth county government building to be located, at this present location, in the county seat of Clarksburg. Completed in 1932 at a cost of $700,000, the five-story buff limestone and polished black granite building occupies the central location in an urban plaza, and reflects its period of construction in the early 20th century.

Harrison County Courthouse
Constructed ~ 1932
Style ~ Art Moderne
County Seat ~ Clarksburg

Located at the midpoint for the Northwestern Turnpike, which ran from Winchester, Virginia to Parkersburg, Harrison County was created in 1784 from a portion of Monongalia County and named for Benjamin Harrison, who was then Governor of Virginia. The first court of Harrison County was held at a private home in Clarksburg on July 20, 1784 and at that meeting, Clarksburg was chosen as the county seat. The town, named for explorer General George Rogers Clark, was chartered in October 1785 and incorporated in 1795.

The Harrison County Courthouse is an excellent example of Art Moderne construction. The vertical spandrel panels at the entrance on the upper floors and the square-headed windows are strong elements of this style. At the cornice level are three roundels; the center one is a clock flanked by relief carvings of the scales of justice. Two bay wings are recessed and flank the entrance bay. The most decorative element is the black granite entrance surround with two metal eagles atop granite chevrons. These were created by sculptor Henry Hering.

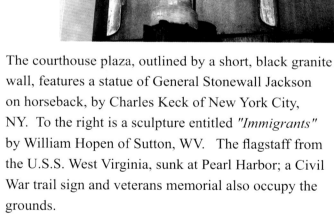

The courthouse plaza, outlined by a short, black granite wall, features a statue of General Stonewall Jackson on horseback, by Charles Keck of New York City, NY. To the right is a sculpture entitled *"Immigrants"* by William Hopen of Sutton, WV. The flagstaff from the U.S.S. West Virginia, sunk at Pearl Harbor; a Civil War trail sign and veterans memorial also occupy the grounds.

The interior of the courthouse is as elegant as the exterior with original Art Moderne features throughout. Black, white and green marble are present as as well as walnut, ebony and mahogany wood. Door fixtures and other hardware in the building are original; elaborate and in the same style as the exterior.

The Division One and Two Circuit Courtrooms have been maintained in the original design and and are quite impressive with both marble and wood elements. The elevated judge's bench and jury boxes, along with the benches and railings are constructed of walnut.

The courtrooms are divided into two sections, one in the rear for the spectators and the other for lawyers, judge, court officers and trial juries. The seating capacity of the two courtrooms varies slightly. Division I (center left) has a capacity of 100, while Division II (bottom right) accommodates 130 spectators.

The jurors are provided with metal foot railings and the spitoons, artifacts of earlier generations, have been preserved in the jury box floor.

Both courtrooms have portraits by American artist, Walter Brough (1890-1978) of Cleveland Ohio; Division I is of John Marshall, the nation's first chief justice of the United States Supreme Court; Edmund Randolph, a distinguished Virginia lawyer and the first Attorney General of the United States overlooks the Division II courtroom.

Jackson County was created from parts of Kanawha, Mason and Wood counties and was named for U.S. President Andrew Jackson, who was in office when the county was formed in 1831.

Ripley, the present county seat, provided a centrally located government for the citizens. The land for the courthouse was the result of a donation by a local family; two acres for the county courthouse and an additional six acres for general public use.

Jackson County Courthouse
Constructed ~ 1918 / 1920
Style ~ Neoclassical Revival
County Seat ~ Ripley

The town was chartered by the Virginia General Assembly in 1832. In that same year, the first courthouse and jail were commissioned to be built. Local history records show that the jail was to be 34 feet by 17 feet, and the courthouse was to be 36 feet square. The one-story brick buildings were completed in 1833 at a cost of $3,700. As the county grew, a larger two-story courthouse was completed in 1858 for $8,993. As the 1858 courthouse aged and became in need of repairs, county officials moved to build the present courthouse, which was completed in 1920.

The current courthouse, located in the downtown is set within a park-like square, and was built over a two-year period at a cost of $125,000. In 1961 an annex and jail were added, at a cost of $350,000, to the rear of the courthouse without impacting the original building.

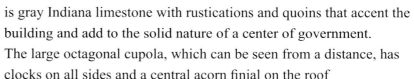

The Neoclassical Revival style building has three stories and a raised basement, which adds to the impressive height of the structure.

The striking facade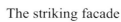
is gray Indiana limestone with rustications and quoins that accent the building and add to the solid nature of a center of government.
The large octagonal cupola, which can be seen from a distance, has clocks on all sides and a central acorn finial on the roof

The entrance is through elevated steps on the basement level which lead to an arcaded entrance bay of rusticated stone. Above the entrance bay is a two-story tall gabled portico supported by large Ionic columns; the facade on the upper floors is smooth stone, flanked by rusticated pilasters.

The gable of the pediment has an ornamental cartouche and the building's name inscribed on the frieze. The basement and first floor windows are simple with stone hoods while the upper story windows have smooth stone surrounds with the third floor having a keystone.

The courtroom, located on the second floor, underwent a 2006 renovation. The balcony is original as is the centrally located judge's bench, and oak benches in the gallery. A mural of the figure of "Justice" is located on the wall behind the judge's bench. It's recessed location is framed by paired, square pilasters with caps and an arched cornice.

The main corridors have retained the decorative mosaic tile flooring and the light fixtures are original.

The courthouse square is completed with multiple memorials. To the left of the courthouse entrance is a monument to Civil War soldiers - the Federal soldiers. A corner of the grounds is reserved for the veterans war memorials - a respectful and well maintained tribute to those who serve their country..

The Greek Revival-style Jefferson County Courthouse is set on a high stone foundation and separated from the street by a modest green-space. It is the county's second courthouse, replacing a small, brick building that was located on the same space within the community.

A view of the second floor courtroom - judges bench.

Jefferson County Courthouse
Constructed ~ 1836
Style ~ Greek Revival
County Seat ~ Charles Town

In 1748, Lord Fairfax, who had a vast holding of land in northern Virginia, sent surveyors to what is now Jefferson County. A young surveyor, George Washington, eventually purchased land a few miles from what is now Charles Town. His brothers, Lawrence, Samuel and Charles also purchased property in the county. The town is named for Charles, who committed that in the event a new county would be formed, that the four corners of the town center be dedicated for public purposes. Shortly after his death in 1799, the new county was formed and in 1801, Charles' son deeded the property to the people.

The entrance to the courthouse dominates the seat of government. A tall portico with four Doric columns and an angular pediment extends across the front of the building. The pediment design is repeated over the windows of the first floor and above the four faces of the clock in the domed tower.

A bronze tablet on the building honors the memory the Confederate veterans of the Civil War..

A small iron balcony accents the space above the front door, and ornamental brackets follow the lines of the eaves.

The present courthouse, while having major changes, retains the basic structure of its 1836 construction. Originally, the ground floor was the courtroom and the site of the trial of John Brown.

In October 1859, Brown led a 21-man contingent against the Federal Armory and Arsenal at Harpers Ferry. Arrested by troop under the command of Col. Robert E. Lee, Brown was charged with murder, inciting slaves to rebel, for murder, and treason against the Commonwealth of Virginia. Found guilty, Brown was sentenced to death by hanging.

Just prior to the Civil War, the court records were moved to Lexington, VA for safekeeping and this was good fortune. During the conflict, Charles Town was frequently occupied by troops, both Union and Confederate. In October 1863, troops and artillery under the command of Confederate General John D. Imboden surrounded Union troops in the courthouse. The brief battle that followed damaged the structure. The building then saw use as a stable and at one point, its roof was removed and used for bullets.

In 1865, the county seat was moved to Shepherdstown and designated as such by the West Virginia Legislature. The new seat of government was established in what is now McMurren Hall, located on the campus of Shepherd University.

McMurren Hall

By 1872, the county seat returned to Charles Town and the war damaged courthouse was restored to the form that we see today. The building was enlarged to accommodate a growing county, including a grand, second-floor courtroom complete with a balcony known as the "ladies listening gallery." The courtroom became home to the West Virginia Supreme Court of Appeals from 1873-1912. During that time, the Supreme Court would ride circuit to Wheeling, Charleston, and Charles Town for one term each year.

In the 1920s, the courthouse was again the location of a high profile treason trial. Miners from southern WV were charged with treason against the state (and some for murder) as a result of the Battle of Blair Mountain in Logan County. The trial received a change of venue to the eastern panhandle in an attempt to find an impartial jury. Following the trials of several of the Battle participants, of which there were only two convictions that were later overturned, the trials again moved to Morgan, Greenbrier and Fayette counties.

The courtroom with its large suspended light and the "ladies" balcony overlooking the proceedings below.

The Kanawha County Courthouse in Charleston is a monumental structure encompassing a city block. With the expanding county needs in the period following Charleston's emergence as the permanent West Virginia State Capital, a grand seat of county government was needed to reflect the growth and success of the county and community.

Kanawha County Courthouse
Constructed ~ 1892
Style ~ Richardsonian Romanesque
County Seat ~ Charleston

Charleston was founded on land that was originally owned by Colonel Thomas Bullitt. In 1774, he was deeded 1,240 acres of land on the Great Kanawha River by the mouth of the Elk River for his service during the French and Indian Wars. The land was eventually sold to Colonel George Clendenin, a frontiersmen and soldier in General Lewis' army at the Battle of Point Pleasant.

Colonel Clendenin, his father Charles, siblings, and six other families moved to the present site of Charleston in 1788 and built the first building within the boundaries of what is now the state capital. The two-story, double log building was known as Clendenin's Fort. The first meeting of the county court took place there on October 5, 1789. The Virginia Assembly chartered the town on December 19, 1794

The building has been the center of Kanawha County government since the date of its erection in 1892, and its site has been the location for all the county courthouses since the formation of Kanawha County in 1789.

Early court records show that tobacco was the legal tender. At the May 1792 court term, it was ordered *"that 4,800 weight of tobacco be levied for extra services of clerk for four years past, and 3,300 weight for extra services performed by Thomas Lewis, Sheriff, from Oct. 5th, 1789 to July 2, 1792."*

The picturesque facade of the Kanawha County Courthouse thus rambles along a full block of Court Street wearing an evenly weathered face of locally quarried stone, and denying, except to a keen observer, the exact location of seams and other structural alterations.

Major additions were constructed in 1917 and 1924 that nearly tripled the original size of the building. This created a series of units tied together by a dominant architectural theme. The result reflected an overall harmony, but still yielded, to the careful observer, individual subtlety of design in each part.

The interior spaces have been altered over the years. The cast iron loggia of the original unit's first floor hallway was enclosed during remodeling work in the 1920s. The outline and detailing, including the intricate capitals, are still visible, although the only remaining free-standing part of the loggia is seen in the stair hall, little changed since 1892. Cast iron rails and newel posts have survived intact.

The textures and details of the interior have been preserved, even to the level of the inlaid tile floors

The stately courtroom is still used for trials that require a large gallery, but the county judicial center now houses court officials and accommodates trials on a daily basis.

The original courtroom on the third floor, encompasses a large space with a high, vaulted ceiling. Ornate chandeliers provide lighting. Beautiful, detailed wood trim is evident throughout the courtroom and in the doorways..

Built in an Italianate style, the Lewis County Courthouse sits upon a slightly elevated lot, which brings attention to the seat of county government. The two-story tall building, which has an almost residential appearance, has a recessed central bay with a tall tower and cupola. A weather vane sits atop the cupola, which has louvered arched openings on each side. The current courthouse is the third permanent courthouse built in Weston and replaces the previous, which burned in 1886.

Lewis County Courthouse
Constructed ~ 1887
Style ~ Italianate
County Seat ~ Weston

Lewis County was created in 1816 from Harrison County, Virginia and named for Colonel Charles Lewis, who was killed in battle at Point Pleasant, in 1774. The first county seat was the town of Westfield, located five miles north of present-day Weston. There, the first meeting of county court was held on March 16, 1817 at a private home.

Weston, which was first known as Preston, then Flesherville, received its present name in 1819, and was incorporated by the West Virginia state legislature in 1913. A stone memorial attests to the early settlement of the area by Henry Flesher and his contribution to the founding of the county.

The courthouse at first seems simple in design, but the main roof has a large cornice with corner brackets and a central metal roof balustrade, creating a much more intricate style. The windows, which are narrow and tall, are square headed with stone hoods. They also have smooth stone sills with corner brackets. A flat-roofed portico, with roof balustrade and paired Doric columns, forms the main entrance. The exterior is complete with two octagonal towers that have pyramidal roofs with metal spire finials. The building has a rusticated stone foundation.

The courthouse grounds are well maintained with a stone wall outlining the lot and two sets of steps access the courthouse entrance. A large granite obelisk dedicated to Lewis County war veterans graces the front lawn and a large, ornamental iron clock sits diagonally from the monument.

The interior of the courthouse has been extensively renovated and the interior offices have modern finishes and configurations.

The courtroom was renovated c. 1978-89. It has a coffered lay-in ceiling, with each square containing a light. Arched recessed panels, with native wood panels between them, consitute the walls. The judge's bench and dividing wall has recessed open wood cells creating a "bee hive" effect. The same wood panels, with the squares cut out, separate the courtroom from the hallway and allow light into the room. Modern, wood benches, with cushioned seats, are provided for the spectator areas. Photographs of the judges, who have served the county, line the walls.

The courthouse is relatively small and as with many counties, additional space is needed; therefore, a new annex building is currently being built to the immediate rear of the historic courthouse.

"The West Virginia County Courthouse is by-and-large the most significant public building in the community with all that it represents. On a broad level, it symbolizes the idea of democracy and local government, while they also embody the traditions and unique historic memory of the state's fifty-five counties. As such, Silling Associates is deeply committed to preserving these priceless resources. It is our passion and pleasure to maintain these cultural icons while also resolving the complex and difficult issues of modern functionality and usefulness." – Thomas M. Potts, President, Silling Associates

right: architect's concept drawing of the new Judicial Center

85

The Lincoln County Courthouse, which was placed into service in 1964, is an example of the architectural style of Modernism. This is the third courthouse in Hamlin and replaces the previous courthouse that was built in 1911.

Lincoln County Courthouse
Constructed ~ 1964
Style ~ Modern / Contemporary
County Seat ~ Hamlin

The Lincoln County Courthouse is a long two-story, flat roofed building of tan/yellow brick with limestone accents, resting upon a granite foundation. The window bays are outlined in limestone for the building's entire height and have keystones which extend up to the limestone band at the cornice level. The entrance is a large limestone frontispiece with "Lincoln County" at the top with metal screening below and a recessed metal framed entrance system. It is five bays wide, and in keeping with its architectural style, has a symmetrical facade and is very severe and streamlined. The interior has maintained its modern design throughout the offices and courtroom.

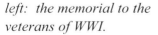

The surrounding courthouse grounds unclutterd, reflecting the building design. There are multiple memorials and benches for the visiting public.

left: the memorial to the veterans of WWI.

right: the memorial to the veterans of WWI, WWII, Korea, and Vietnam

The second county courthouse - built in 1911.

Lincoln County was the third county to be formed following West Virginia's statehood. Created by an an act of the West Virginia Legislature on February 23, 1867, it was formed from parts of Cabell, Putnam, Kanawha and Boone counties. The new county was named for U.S. President, Abraham Lincoln.

In an excerpt from the records - "*Be it enacted by the Legislature of West Virginia: ... a new county, which shall be called and known by the name of the County of Lincoln, in honor of our late chief magistrate, who paid his life as a forfeit for his devotion to our glorious Union.*"

The first meeting of the Board of Supervisors was held on the 11th day of March, 1867, in what was known as Hamlin Chapel, an old church which stood on a farm, less than one mile from present-day Hamlin. It was there that officials announced that White Hall, a Southern Methodist Church, which was ¼ mile from the present county seat, was to hold the first sessions of court in the county. White Hall was occupied by soldiers during the Civil War and at the end of the fighting it was heavily damaged. Authorities took possession of it at that time and it was used as a courthouse from 1867 until 1875. The trustees of the church repurchased the building in 1875.

below: the entry walls are covered in highly polished marble

The courtroom is richly adorned with oak in the wall panels, seating, litigation well and the judges bench.

The current courthouse is the fourth courthouse in Logan and is located on the same site as the previous. Built at a cost of one million dollars, it is constructed in the Brutalist style of architecture, which was a popular Modern style in the 1960s.

Located in the southern part of the state, Logan County was created in 1824 from parts of Giles, Tazewell, Cabell and Kanawha counties, Virginia. It was named for Chief Logan of the Mingo tribe.

LOGAN COUNTY COURTHOUSE

While the courthouse grounds are not much larger than the building itself, careful consideration has been given to the landscaping to create a pleasant and colorful envionment.

Logan County Courthouse
Constructed ~ 1964 / 1965
Style ~ Modern / Contemporary
County Seat ~ Logan

Located on the Guyandotte River, the present county seat was first known by explorers of the 1780s as "Islands of the Guyandot." It was named Lawnsville, in 1827, after Anthony Lawson, who built a trading post in the area. In 1853, it was chartered as Aracoma, for the daughter of Chief Logan, by Virginia's General Assembly. When the U.S. Post Office established the first mail route, the town was known as Logan Courthouse. This remained until 1907, when the town received its present name of Logan.

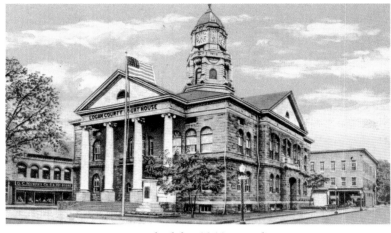
postcard of the 1911 courthouse

All early court records were destroyed May 1, 1864, when a detachment of the 42nd Ohio Infantry Regiment, under Brigadier-General Averil, burned the courthouse. In 1870, a brick courthouse was constructed and it was in service until 1904, when it was replaced. The courthouse burned in 1911, and the $40,000 insurance was used towards the construction of a courthouse which had an approximate cost of $63,000. After falling into disrepair, it was replaced by the courthouse we see today.

The four-story, flat-roofed building has a first floor facade of polished black granite and is recessed back from the upper two floors, adding dimension to the structure. The upper two floors, which are metal paneled, project from the first and fourth floor. The fourth floor, which was built as a jail, is yellow brick. While the building has no ornamentation, which is consistent with the architectural style, it has a mix of materials, which provides the onlooker with a visually interesting seat of county government. The interior is well maintained and also modern in design.

Brutalist architecture came into the public eye from the 1950s to the mid-1970s, as an outgrowuth of the modernist architectural movement. Building, such as the Logan County Courthouse, are typically very linear, blockish and fortress-like. Concrete is often the predominant choice of construction material. Initially the style came about for government buildings and other structures that needed to be functional for the public and at a low cost.

left: vertical panel wall sections extend beyond the core structure adding an exaggerated dimensional quality.

below: the conventional brick section of the top level houses the jail.

The courtroom is simple and modern in style, yet very functional, reflecting the overall design of the building.

The modern courtroom honors the past with photographs of the previous judges that line the walls.

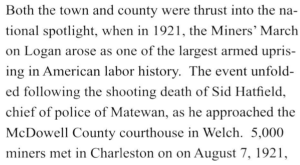

Thomas H. Harvey 1897-1905; J.B. Wilkenson 1905-1916; Robert Bland 1920-1928 are a few of the past judges that adorn the walls of the courtroom.

Both the town and county were thrust into the national spotlight, when in 1921, the Miners' March on Logan arose as one of the largest armed uprising in American labor history. The event unfolded following the shooting death of Sid Hatfield, chief of police of Matewan, as he approached the McDowell County courthouse in Welch. 5,000 miners met in Charleston on on August 7, 1921, to present demands to Governor Morgan. Miners began to assemble near Charleston to prepare a march south to overthrow the governor's proclamation of martial law in Mingo County and remove anti-union mine guard and deputy sheriff systems in Logan and Mingo counties.

With Union leader Bill Blizzard as field commander, the Miners March began on August 24. The following day, the miners arrived at Blair Mountain in northern Logan County, where they were met by Sheriff Don Chafin and armed forces. By September 1, the miners were ready to descend upon Logan, now occupied by federal troops. With the presence of the troops, the miners agreed to lay down their guns.

Following the unrest of unionization, Logan continued to grow and became a major hub of economic activity in its region of the state.

U.S. Army soldiers pose by a supply train in Logan.

The Marion County Courthouse, located in the central business district of Fairmont, is a display of grand architecture. The monumental size of the domed courthouse, combined with expansive approaches to the seat of county government, reflects the emergence of Fairmont and Marion County as a major center of commerce and industry at the beginning of the 20th century

Marion County Courthouse
Constructed ~ 1897 / 1900
Style ~ Beaux Arts
County Seat ~ Fairmont

The original Marion County Courthouse

The first Marion County Courthouse, of brick construction, was built in the Greek Revival style with a portico and belfry. It served the county for fifty-three years but was considered too small by county leaders, as Fairmont became the center of a vast coal and gas producing industry, and Marion County increased in population and prosperity. This growth prompted the county officials to consider plans for a new and larger courthouse by 1893. Not all Fairmont residents were in support of the expenditure for a new courthouse and the construction of a new building did not seem possible until one event took place.

The renovation or replacement of a courthouse is a serious and often, expensive process. However, in 1897, a group of citizens in the county decided to provide free labor to settle the issue of whether or not to build a new courthouse. As reported by the local newspaper, a mob of about eighty men, armed with crowbars, axes and mattocks, and apparently incited by local officials (and possibly with the aid of whiskey) who desired a finer courthouse, damaged the courthouse. The paper officially reported that " a short time after the court adjourned in the evening, a large force of men was put to work and by midnight they had torn away the rear portion of the first story." The editor further stated that "there is considerable opposition throughout the county to this action of the court, but as everybody in the county knows we need a new building, it is thought the objections will soon be withdrawn."

The result of the demolition of the county's first courthouse, is the building that we see today.

The unofficial courthouse demolition crew took time to pose for a photograph atop the rubble of the nights work.

left: construction is underway on the new courthouse.

The main entrance has a hexastyle portico and is approached by a broad, two-flight stair accented with four metal lamps and stone balustrades. The columns support an entablature with a detailed frieze. The pediment is detailed and sculptures representing justice, power, agriculture and mining. Near the apex of the pediment, an eagle with outstretched wings signifies power and just below the eagle is the Scales of Justice. In the right corner of the pediment a mining car, a shovel, and the figure of a man represent the coal mining interests of the county and the state.

A small dome carried above a high dome dominates the character of the Marion County Courthouse. Its four principal sides are pedimented and centered with clock faces. The belvedere of the richly figured dome is surmounted by a large figure holding the Scales of Justice.

The Division 1 Circuit Courtroom is rich in classical detail. The courtroom, containing a judge's dais, seating and a balcony is flanked on each side with four Ionic columns. A large stained-glass dome is centered above the seating of the courtroom.

The courthouse dome houses an inner dome that forms the rotunda, two stories in height, from which major interior corridors open. The corridor roofs are barrel-vaulted and contain twenty-five coffers, nine of which are filled with stained glass. The rotunda dome is an elaborate, sixteen-panel stained glass skylight.

right: the rotunda dome.

A view of the balcony and the courtroom below.

The courthouse sits within the Moundsville Commercial Historic District. Built originally in the Romanesque style, it has been altered to become the Colonial Revival building we see today. The style is evident with the tall, two-story entrance portico with pediment, the roof cupola, and red brick facade.

Marshall County Courthouse
Constructed ~ 1876
Style ~ Colonial Revival
County Seat ~ Moundsville

Moundsville, the county seat, was named for the Grave Creek Indian Mound which is located in the heart of the town. The town, as its exists today, was originally two separate towns; Elizabethtown and Moundsville which were consolidated in 1866.

The first settler to the region was Joseph Tomlinson in 1770, who laid out Elizabethtown in 1798, which is the northern section of present-day Moundsville. Named for Tomlinson's wife, Elizabethtown encompassed only 45 acres. The first lot sold in 1799 and the town was incorporated in 1803. Tomlinson died in 1825 and shortly thereafter his widow laid out an addition fronting the river, and in 1832 this addition was incorporated into Elizabethtown. The population at that time was about 300 persons. The same year, Simon Purdy incorporated the town of Moundsville on land he had purchased in 1831 that was adjacent to Elizabethtown, to the south.

Both towns were originally located in Ohio County. Marshall County was not formed until 1835. The location of the county seat was hotly contested. Joesph Tomlinson had petitioned the government in Richmond, in 1808, to appoint Elizabethtown as the Ohio County seat, but it was defeated. Petitioning continued until 1832 when a committee was

above: two earlier views of the current courthouse - note the addition of a portico in the later, bottom photo.

appointed to the select the site of the county seat; the committee selected Elizabethtown, but the county court refused to comply. Marshall County was subsequently formed in 1835 due to this strife and Elizabethtown was recognized as the county seat and the first courthouse was selected in 1836.

The county was named in honor of John Marshall, Secretary of State under President Thomas Jefferson, and Chief Justice of the United States Supreme Court. The Marshall County Court was organized in 1835 in a school building in Elizabethtown at what is now the corner of First Street and Baker Avenue, Moundsville. The original courthouse was erected in Elizabethtown in 1836 at a cost of $4200. It was two stories high and contained the jail. This first courthouse was used for 39 years until the present courthouse was built in 1876 for a cost of $27,740. The present courthouse was constructed following Elizabethtown and Moundsville merger to become Moundsville in 1866.

While the central structure dates from 1876, the building has been renovated: the original corner towers and front entrance have been removed, the painted brick was stripped, and an addition was added in the 1970s, creating the current Colonial Revival architectural style.

The courthouse is part of a large town square that is populated with a variety of memorials.

A Civil War monument stands at the corner of the Courthouse lawn flanked by two restored Civil War cannons. At the side of the building is a fountain and monument dedicated to the memory of all war veterans.

MEDAL OF HONOR
Benjamin C. Criswell, Sergeant, Company B,
7th U.S. Cavalry, United States Army

CITATION

Rescued the body of 2nd Lieutenant Benjamin H. Hodgson from within the enemy lines; brought up ammunition and encouraged the men in the most exposed positions under heavy fire in the Little Big Horn River fight.
Sergeant Benjamin C. Criswell received the Medal of Honor on October 5, 1878 for his actions on the Little Big Horn River, Montana, on June 25, 1876. Sergeant Criswell was born on February 9, 1849 in Moundsville, Virginia (West Virginia) and enlisted in the United States Army at age 21 on May 31, 1870 in Cincinnati, Ohio. He was wounded in the neck in the fighting on the Little Big Horn River on June 25, 1876. He was discharged from U. S. Army service on April 3, 1878 as a First Sergeant of excellent character. He died on October 17, 1921 and is buried at Pleasant Hill Cemetery, Eldorado, Oklahoma.
This plaque is dedicated to the memory of the patriotic service of a brave soldier from Marshall County by the Marshall County Commission on Memorial Day, May 31, 1999.

R. E. "Slim Lehart" Hartley   President
Donald K. Mason   Commissioner
H. L. "Biggie" Byard   Commissioner

Two walls in the main entryway are dedicated to honoring those who served in the military from Marshall County

Located near the Civil War Memorial is a small plaque dedicated to a recipient of the Medal of Honor for his heroic actions with the 7th Cavalry at the Little Big Horn in 1876.

The second floor houses a modern and spacious courtroom.

The Mason County Courthouse a tri-level stone structure with a smooth limestone facade, is constructed in the style of Modernism. Originally costing about $750,000, it was completed in 1957. This is Mason County's third courthouse in the only county seat, Point Pleasant.

Mason County Courthouse
Constructed ~ 1956 / 1957
Style ~ Modern / Contemporary
County Seat ~ Point Pleasant

Mason County was created by an act of the Virginia General Assembly on January 2, 1804, from parts of Kanawha County. The county was named in honor of George Mason, the author of the Constitution of Virginia, and a member of the Philadelphia Constitutional Convention that framed the Constitution of the United States.

The county seat of Point Pleasant was originally chartered in 1794 and incorporated 1833. Located on the mouth of the Kanawha River, it was named after Camp Point Pleasant, established by General Andrew Lewis at the time of his battle with the Indians in 1774. The first courthouse was a log building typical of the time period. Prior to the construction of the current courthouse, the seat of county government was located in a courthouse that stood for nearly 100 years, which was built at a cost of approximately $5000.

The expansive entry is bright and open - it makes navigation to the various county offices easy.

A portrait of George Mason, namesake of the county, hangs in the stairway to the second floor.

The Point Pleasant Register in October, 1958, provided remembrances of that courthouse. *"Although razed only four years ago, citizens seldom have occasion today to recall the days when a sidewalk from Main Street though 6th Street cut diagonally across the court house park and it was difficult to spend a few hours in town without walking over the burial place of the ill-fated Chief Cornstalk, or around his monument that formed the hub of the park. There were the days when the county offices were strewn over a considerable area, the days before a person could be arrested, indicted, tried, convicted, and jailed, all under one roof."*

99

There is one myth about the Mason County Courthouse that the County Clerk's office often addresses; is it has never burned nor suffered the loss of records. The story seems to originate from an incident when there was an explosion in the jail in 1976, which was part of the courthouse at that time. A man came to visit his wife, who was accused of murder. He carried a bag of explosives and a gun. The tragedy that followed left five people dead, including the sheriff and two deputies. The jail was destroyed and rebuilt, but left cracks in the floors of the courthouse.

The large courtroom is a unique festival of wood parque panels and accents, creating an inviting and interestingly professional atmosphere - certainly in keeping with the overall modern design of the building.

Point Pleasant saw conflict during the Civil War. There are historical accounts that the courthouse served as headquarters for Union Company Commander Captain J.D. Carter, and a large amount of supplies was reported to have been stored in the building. Confederate General Albert Gallatin Jenkins and his troops entered the city and attempted to rout the Union troops from their position in the courthouse in an exchange that lasted close to four hours. The Confederate troops failed when reinforcements arrived from Gallipolis.

Like many communities across the state, the street signs clearly announce that you are near the courthouse.

When the modern courthouse was dedicated in October 1958, the local newspaper described several of the features for the new building, *"One wing, houses the jail and jailer's quarters. In a brick penthouse atop the building are the sheriff's living quarters, consisting of three bedrooms, two baths, living and dining room, and kitchen. In the penthouse, too is a guestroom, study, and bath to be used by visiting dignitaries."* It was also noted that the new building had 55 rooms and approximately 665,000 bricks were used in its construction.

The McDowell County Courthouse is a commanding sight on the courthouse lawn, overlooking the the county seat of Welch. Even with the addition of numerous buildings in the town since the time of its construction, the elevation provides the citizenry with an unobstructed view of their chief public building.

The original unit of the courthouse is a two and one-half story building with a square three-story tower at its northeast corner. The exterior wall surfaces are of native, rock-faced stone and the roofs are covered

with slate. In 1909 an addition was built at the north elevation, also in a Romanesque style with identical materials. The two units are joined by a connecting wing with an open under-pass flanked on either side by Romanesque-style columns.

McDowell County Courthouse
Constructed ~ 1893 / 1894
Style ~ Romanesque Revival
County Seat ~ Welch

McDowell County was created by an act of the Virginia General Assembly on February 28, 1858, from parts of Tazewell County, Virginia. The county was named in honor of James McDowell, the 25th Governor of Virginia.

The act creating the county specified that the county seat was to be located at Perryville, and the initial meetings of the county court where held there. The construction of a courthouse, jail and other

top right: postcard of the courthouse in the configuration we see today. above: the early courthouse without the additions.

public buildings was delayed. However, due to a dispute concerning the ownership of the site selected, the delay extended through the Civil War years, with the court meetings taking place throughout the county.

In 1867, the West Virginia state legislature passed a law locating the county seat near Coalwood. Then, in 1872 the state legislature allowed the county residents to select the location of the county seat and they chose Perryville, the largest town in the county at the time.

Population centers began to shift with the coming of the Norfolk and Western Railroad into the southern coal fields of the state. The tracks reached McDowell County in 1886 and the coal industry boomed with activity and brought jobs and workers with their families to the county. During the 1890s, the population around the town of Welch increased, and the citizens of the town demanded that they have the county seat. In 1892, a county-wide vote resulted in Welch being named the new county seat.

With the developing economy of the coal fields that permitted the erection of a substantial courthouse at Welch, there were undercurrents of labor unrest that surfaced in the union organizing movement of the early 1920's.

On August 1, 1921, as Sid Hatfield and a companion, Edward Chambers, walked the steps of the McDowell County Courthouse, they were shot and killed by agents of the coal companies. The shooting was given wide coverage in the national press, and is credited with increasing the disorder which led to the Battle of Blair Mountain and the miners March on Logan.

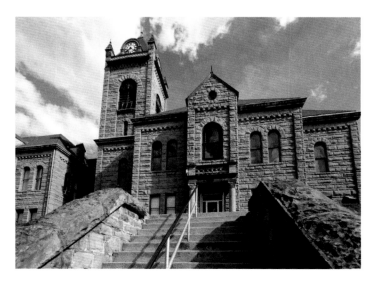

Some of the interior elements have remained over the years. The main stairway is of heavy cast iron, including treads, newels, and rails. The open-well, two-flight stair extends to the courtroom which occupies the entire upper floor of the original section of the courthouse.

With its corner spires, the central clock tower has a genuine castle-like quality which dominates the building.

The courtroom has been remodeled with a light wood paneling in contrast to the dark wood of the spectator seating. The jury box, which is large enough to seat a "grand jury", is arranged on different levels to provide each juror full access to the proceedings.

Art Deco style architecture is elegantly displayed in the design of the Mercer County Courthouse. The central section of the building has slender, 2-story windows and square, engaged columns that create an emphasis on the vertical design. While there is little exterior ornamentation, the geometric shapes and ribbed surfaces create a visually appealing view and conveys the image of a solid seat of local government.

Mercer County Courthouse
Constructed ~ 1930 / 1931
Style ~ Art Deco
County Seat ~ Princeton

Mercer County was created by an act of the Virginia General Assembly on March 17, 1837, from parts of Giles and Tazewell Counties Virginia. The county was named in honor of Brigadier General Hugh Mercer, who served in the American Revolutionary War and was mortally wounded at the Battle of Princeton, New Jersey, 1777.

The courthouse as it appeared about 1890-1900.

The first meeting of the county court took place at a private home near the present site of Princeton. There it was decided to name the county seat Princeton, in honor of the site of General Mercer's death. One and a half acres of land for the courthouse was donated by a local resident, Capt. William Smith.

A conflict arose over the location of the county seat in 1865. Princeton residents would not allow the judge, Nathaniel Harrison, to hold court in the town, primarily because he had left the Confederacy. As a result, he held the county court at Concord Church, present-day Athens, for five years following the war.

In 1869, Princeton residents reportedly stole the county court records to return them to Princeton. A special election was then held in the county to resolve the issue, and Princeton was successful in being named the county seat. Briefly, in the early 1900s there was a rivalry for the county seat again, this time with Bluefield, which had become a thriving community with the growth of the coal industry. This dispute was resolved with an election in 1907, in which Princeton received enough votes to remain as the county seat.

Mercer County's present courthouse, built in 1930-31, is the sixth buildings that has served the county as the seat of government. It replaced the one built in 1875. Two courthouses were lost to fires; one was destroyed during the Civil War by a blaze that was set by Confederates, and the fourth, built in 1874, was burned to the ground in a suspicious fire a year later.

Located to the right of the courthouse is the county judicial center annex.

An an aerial view shows how the current courthouse is situated in the community. It actually sits in what amounts to a traffic circle. There are entrances on each north/south end of the building, although at present, the north entrance serves as the primary entry point. The massive art deco design is clearly evident. It is a beautiful example of this style of design.

The windows have flanking ribbed borders that form Deco motifs in the two-story recessed panels of the front-facing wings. On the side elevation, an idealized carved relief, depicting a shield, decorates each spandrel (panel) between the first and second floor windows.

Flanking the carved surround at both the north and south entrances is a richly carved frieze representing phases in the historical development of the county. The design for the carvings are credited to Mrs. S.L. Mahood, mother of the architect.

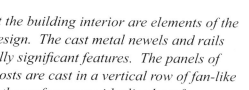

The brass, entrance doorways are recessed, with the inscription, "*Justice Is The Right Of All The People.*"

The main doors to the courtroom are covered in leather with brass, hob-nail accents.

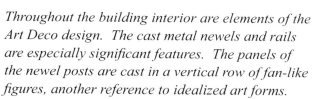

Throughout the building interior are elements of the Art Deco design. The cast metal newels and rails are especially significant features. The panels of the newel posts are cast in a vertical row of fan-like figures, another reference to idealized art forms.

The courtroom is large with dark, wood paneling and carved wood trim. Sound control panels are fitted to the walls to reduce reverberation during proceedings.

The decor of the courtrooms echoes the strong, uncluttered lines of the exterior.

Mineral County Courthouse
Constructed ~ 1868
Style ~ Romanesque Revival
County Seat ~ Keyser

Located in Keyser, the Mineral County Courthouse occupies a small lot and is surrounded with a grassy lawn. Three eras of construction created this building. The original section of the courthouse, a two-and-one-half story brick building, was completed in 1868. A three-story, Romanesque Revival addition on the main elevation of the courthouse provides the principal exterior design we see today.

The area that is now Mineral County was part of the lands of Lord Fairfax, who had it surveyed in 1848 to locate the source of the Potomac River, which was the western limit of his holdings. The formation of the county, originally part of Hampshire County, came when Henry Gassaway Davis arrived in the community of New Creek (now know as Keyser). He worked with the B&O Railroad prior to the Civil War, but left his position as a brakeman to begin a business selling railroad ties to the Union Army.

By 1865, Davis acquired a large area of land that would become the county seat. Davis and his colleagues wanted Hampshire County to be divided so there would be a courthouse closer to his business interests. The state legislature accommodated the railroad builder's request.

In developing the town, Davis had his land surveyed into six hundred lots and sold them for about $300 each, netting a profit of $200,000. Davis offered a site for a courthouse which was accepted by the county court. He used the land donation to secure New Creek (Keyser), as the county seat. The name of the community was changed from New Creek to Keyser in 1874 in honor of the B & O's Vice-President, William Keyser.

The third story of the tower features an arched transom with stone surrounds and keystone. A large circular vent with decorative stone surround is located above the third story and is repeated on the side elevations of the tower. In addition to the tower, the 1895 addition features a stone base and corner quoins. A cornice of decorative brickwork tops each elevation. Small, two-story, brick additions were constructed to each side of the original building as well as the rear c.1955.

A veterans memorial on the front lawn commemorates local veterans of World War I and II, the Korea War, and Vietnam. It was moved to the courthouse in 1967 from a park. A memorial dedicated to the memory of local law enforcement officials has also been erected in front of the courthouse building.

The second floor courtroom has a gable ceiling with exposed rafters, decorative brackets, acoustical tiles, and suspended fluorescent lighting. An outstanding feature is the mahogany, judges bench, which is accented with large, matching wood panels. Flanking the bench is a pair of pilasters topped with a decorative cornice. Jury seating is situated in the south corner of the room and a solid wood bannister separates the court area from the gallery which contains four rows of bench seating.

The wood trim in the courtroom is decorated with a variety of intricate carvings. An admonition for justice adorns the panel behind the judge's bench, while the witness chair boasts a carving of a rising sun.

The courthouse is Modern in style with elements from Art Deco and Art Moderne. The four-story, flat-roofed building, with a dark polished granite base, has a facade of smooth Indiana limestone and features fluted pilasters across the front dividing the bays. These pilasters support a smooth stone entablature. Dark granite spandrels separate the floors between the windows and dark granite surrounds the entrance. The top floor is set back and was constructed as the jail.

A veterans memorial sits at the corner of the courthouse.

Mingo County Courthouse
Constructed ~ 1966
Style ~ Modern / Contemporary
County Seat ~ Williamson

FRANK P. MILBURN,
Architect.

MINGO COUNTY COURT HOUSE.
During Construction.

Williamson, W. Va.

Mingo County was created from Logan County, West Virginia in 1895 and is the youngest county in the state. The current courthouse is the county's second. The first was built circa 1904 at the same site. Located on street level on Courthouse Square, it is in the heart of downtown Williamson, the county seat.

left: a photo of the construction of the first courthouse showing the framework for the central tower, which is unfinished.

Williamson is located on the Tug Fork of the Big Sandy River. The town rests on the state line, across from South Williamson, Kentucky. It was named for the Williamson family, who were prominent in the community and provided the property for the courthouse. The site was farmland as late as 1890, but was transformed as the Norfolk & Western Railway (now Norfolk Southern) built its main line through the area. It was designated as the center of county government when Mingo County was formed. Officially incorporated in 1905, by a special charter of the legislature, the town boomed with the growth and development of the local coalfields.

above: a view of the completed courthouse from a hand-colored postcard photo.

Williamson was the site of a high-profile trial in 1921 that took place in the original courthouse. Sid Hatfield, the sheriff of Matewan, and 17 other men were tried for murders that resulted from a gun battle with agents of the coal company - all men were acquitted. The event, known as the Matewan Massacre, is often cited as the beginning of the West Virginia Mine War of 1920-21, which escalated into an armed conflict. Presiding over the trial was Judge Robert Darius "R. D." Bailey, who served the Mingo County circuit court from 1921 to 1928.

R. D. Bailey

Bailey also oversaw another prominent case in Mingo County court. In the murder trial of Levi Lane and Clyde Beale, the jury failed to recommend mercy, and handed down the sentence of death by hanging. While Beale's appeal was pending at the state Supreme Court, Bailey learned that he had been convicted on per-

above: the Matewan defendants posing in front of the courthouse.

jured testimony. Despite orders from the Supreme Court, Bailey refused to set a date for Beale's hanging, since he was convinced that a miscarriage of justice had taken place in his court. Beale's sentence was later commuted to life imprisonment, and in 1949 Beale was pardoned by Governor Patteson.

The courtroom is contemporary in style with a traditional layout. On the wall behind the judges bench, the Great Seal of Mingo County is on display. The seal features images that represent the first courthouse and the significance of the mining, timber, and railroad industries in the history of the county.

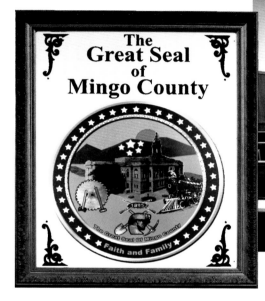

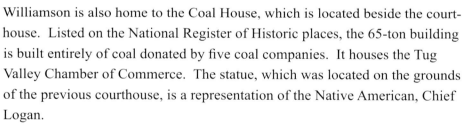

Williamson is also home to the Coal House, which is located beside the courthouse. Listed on the National Register of Historic places, the 65-ton building is built entirely of coal donated by five coal companies. It houses the Tug Valley Chamber of Commerce. The statue, which was located on the grounds of the previous courthouse, is a representation of the Native American, Chief Logan.

The Monongalia County Courthouse, located in downtown Morgantown, is an excellent example of nineteenth century architecture, and is an historical and architectural landmark in the community. Constructed in 1891 for $53,478.00 the builders laid the cornerstone on June 20, 1891, West Virginia Day.

Monongalia County Courthouse
Constructed ~ 1891
Style ~ Romanesque Revival
County Seat ~ Morgantown

Monongalia County was one of three counties created by an act of the Virginia General Assembly in October 1776 from the District of West Augusta, Virginia. Morgantown, the county seat, was incorporated as the Borough of Morgantown by the Virginia General Assembly on February 3, 1838. The town grew slowly until the Baltimore and Ohio Railroad arrived in the city on February 14, 1886.

The early development of Morgantown was directly related to the courthouse. Businesses and residents saw the advantages of locating near the center of county government activity. In addition to the courthouse serving as a place for public meetings, the courtyard in front of the building has been the site of street fairs, markets, political rallies and protests, and concerts.

above: a view of the original courthouse

This courthouse replaced a two-story brick structure which was completed in 1848. In 1884, the old courthouse was declared dangerous. Due to opposition by county residents, the county court postponed plans for a new courthouse. In 1887, the court hired an architect for $25.00 to make plans for a new courthouse. County residents continued to be in favor of repairing of the existing building.

The courthouse deteriorated beyond repair and the county officials resorted to drastic measures to reach their goal of a new courthouse. On September 13, 1890 at midnight, county officials removed the records from the courthouse and ordered its demolition. By the next morning, the building demolition was well underway. Citizens sought a court injunction to halt further work but during the night, the circuit court officials had apparently left town.

The result was the courthouse we see today. It is a two-story building with five-story clock tower and three-story South tower. A common bond pattern of red brick covers the exterior with stone belt courses. These top the sandstone basement and proivde a visual, horizontal division between the various sections of the building.

The courtyard was the site of the public whipping post, stocks and pillories until 1818. Presently, it is the site of three monuments to the veterans and those who lost their lives in of America's wars.

above: the Seal of Monongalia County is displayed on the rear wall of the court-room, while the state seal adorns the wall behind the judges bench.

The Circuit Courtroom is modern in style. It is very open and well designed for both spectators and citizens with business before the court. The use of plants adds comfort and color to the surroundings.

right: At the time of publication, Jean Friend, Clerk of the Circuit and Family courts, is the longest serving clerk in the state. She has been elected to and served nine consecutive terms in the office.

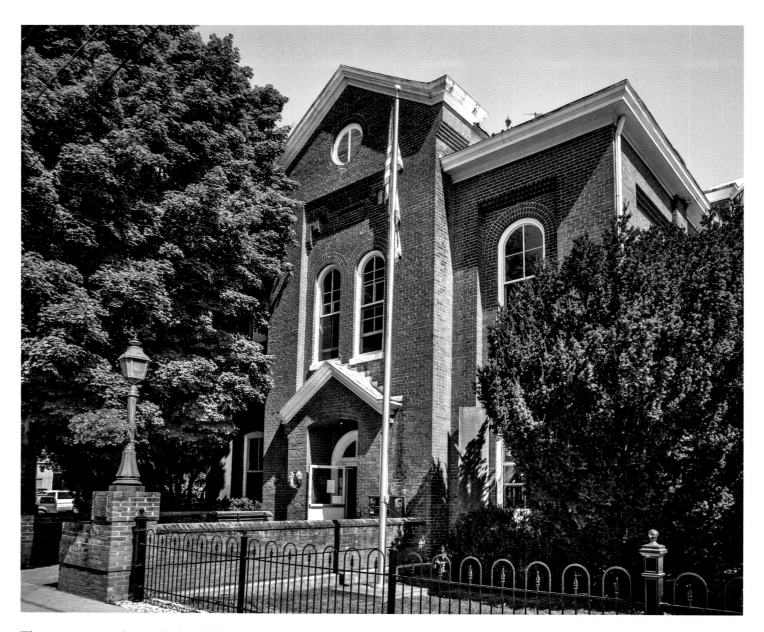

The current courthouse is the third in Union and was built in 1882 in the Romanesque Revival style. It is known that the bricks used in the construction were locally manufactured and that all three courthouses in Union were constructed in the same location. The central entrance is within a small gabled, projecting bay. Paired windows are located immediately above it.

Monroe County Courthouse
Constructed ~ 1882
Style ~ Romanesque Revival
County Seat ~ Union

The Monroe County Courthouse, while appearing simple in design, reveals many details upon close observation. It is a two-story, hip roof building with projecting two-story gable bays on each elevation, except for the rear. The roof is metal and has a decorative metal roof balustrade. The facade is red brick and is accented with corbelling at the edge of the bays and across the top of the main section. The gable bays have circular windows with circular brick surrounds. First-floor windows are semi-elliptical and have semi-elliptical brick arches and smooth stone sills while the windows on the second floor have a brick hood and smooth stone sills.

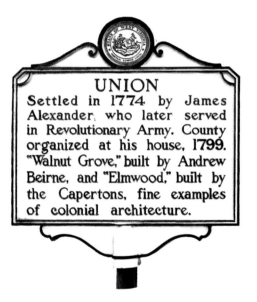

UNION
Settled in 1774 by James Alexander who later served in Revolutionary Army. County organized at his house, 1799. "Walnut Grove," built by Andrew Beirne, and "Elmwood," built by the Capertons, fine examples of colonial architecture.

Union, the present county seat, was settled in 1774 by James Alexander. The land, which he donated, was the site of the first and subsequent courthouses. A survey completed in 1774 indicated that there were 54 families living in the county at that time. The town was named Union for the rendezvous site where the troops would gather (forming a union) during the French and Indian Wars.

In 1790, Greenbrier County was faced with a territory battle that lasted for over a decade. Monroe County petitioned in 1795 to break away from Greenbrier County. Among the chief complaints, were that the courthouse was too far away and the Greenbrier River was a natural barrier between the two tracts of land.

The requests to Richmond were fruitful, and Monroe County was created in 1799 from Greenbrier County. It was named for United State President, James Monroe. The town of Union was was chartered by the Virginia General Assembly that same year.

According to the national census of 1800, Monroe County had a population of 4,188, the 9th largest population of the 13 counties then in existence in the present state of West Virginia. This growth was in part due to Monroe and Greenbrier counties serving as the settlement gateway into West Virginia from the Valley of the Virginias. The area seems to develop quickly. Records show that the first merchant in the town opened doors for business in 1800. The town's postmaster was named that same year. In 1802, Charles Friend opened the town's first hotel. The town was incorporated under the State of West Virginia in 1868.

Early court records provide some insight as to the workings of the judicial system around the turn of the 18th century.

From 1800: *"Sheriff to have stocks and pillary built; Patrick Boyd given a peddler's license; For outrageous drunkness, abusing the court, cursing in their presence, threatening mischief, Dennis Cochran is fined $28 and sent to jail until quiet and ready to confess his fault."*

above: part of the old jail - now used as storage and preparation space for voting machines.

The arched windows of the courtroom provide considerable natural lighting, supplemented by the modern, ceiling fixtures.

The interior of the courthouse has been somewhat altered through time but many of the original interior elements remain such as the woodwork, wainscoting and metal and wood staircases.

The long corridors are not without their amenities. Bench seating is provided and numerous photographs and other decorative touches line the walls. The combination of the green wainscoting and the oak flooring give a feeling of the simple elegance of an earlier era.

The current courthouse is located on the corner of Washington and Fairfax Streets, and is the fourth courthouse in Berkeley Springs. Dedicated in 2010, it replaces the previous courthouse that was destroyed by fire in 2006. While the building was a loss, the records were saved by a fireproof vault room and lines of volunteers, who passed them hand to hand to waiting trucks to be relocated for safe keeping.

Morgan County Courthouse
Constructed ~ 2010
Style ~ Modern / Contemporary
County Seat ~ Berkeley Springs

Morgan County was formed in 1820 from portions of Hampshire and Berkeley counties, Virginia and named for Revolutionary War soldier, General Daniel Morgan. The incorporated name of the county seat is Bath, but it is commonly known as Berkeley Springs for the mineral springs, which still flows today. George Washington came to Berkeley Springs in 1748 to enjoy of the warm spring water.

above: the courthouse as it appeared on a postcard in 1889.

The Morgan County court met for the first time in Bath on March 16, 1820 in Ignatious O'Ferrall's tavern. Later meetings were held at the Buck Horn Tavern until a building was purchased for the court's use. Court officials purchased a stone house for the sole purpose of a courthouse on the corner of Wilkes and Fairfax Streets. In 1844, a fire destroyed many of the downtown's buildings including the courthouse. Two years later, the county sold the land back to the original owners and purchased the current courthouse lot at Washington and Fairfax Streets.

News reports indicate the central place in community life the courthouse played. In 1883 it was reported that "*Sheriff Buzzerd has treated the Courthouse to a thorough cleaning, a new carpet etc., and it looks very respectable. We think the tobacco chewers should let up spitting over the new carpet for a year at least.*" Nearly a decade later there was a move to upgrade the courthouse, with some citizens suggesting that new property be purchased to create a courthouse grounds, but officials chose to remain at the same location.

At the turn of the 20th century, the remodeling of the third courthouse involved the removal of the portico and alterations to the tower cupola. A clock was inserted in the tower, which was sold to the county by a local jeweler in 1908.

According to newspaper accounts, the clock had an illuminated dial and four faces of four feet diameter. The "newly remodeled" third courthouse opened on September 5, 1908. It was described as "light colored pressed brick with sandstone trimmings surmounted by a well proportioned clock and tower." Additions were completed in 1923 and 1953.

right: in 2006, the courthouse was destroyed by fire.

The architectural style is a modern adaptation of the previous courthouse style. A large, three-story corner block with two short tiers above capped with a cupola. The cupola has clock faces on each facade and a metal roof topped with a metal spire. The facade is smooth stone with irregular cut stone accents. The main structure features a tall arched entrance bay on two sides.

The interior of the courthouse is done in very light tones to give a feeling of openness and light. The light colored walls and wood work are carried thought the corridors, offices and courtroom. The courtroom is modern with light colored wood and carpet throughout.

The interior hallways are wide and bright with a combination of ceiling lights and large window areas.

below: the bell, that was housed in the cupola of the old courthouse and salvaged from the fire, is on display.

A display, in the hallway opposite the entrance to the Circuit Courtroom, houses replicas of the Declaration of Independence and the U.S. Constitution.

The courthouse is located on Courthouse Square in the center of Summersville. Set back from the street with a broad lawn in front, and a sandstone wall around the lot, it was constructed in 1898. In the 1940s, a rear addition was financed through the Works Progress Administration (WPA).

The War Memorial honors veterans from WWI, WWII, and Vietnam.

Nicholas County Courthouse
Constructed ~ 1896 / 1898
Style ~ Neoclassical Revival
County Seat ~ Summersville

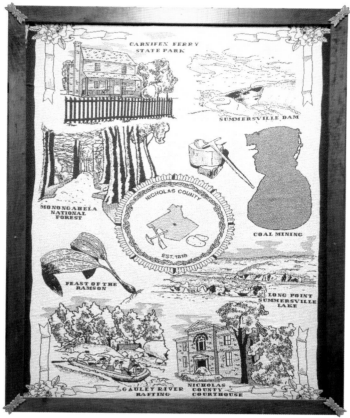

A weaving, depicting significant elements in the history of the county, adorns the wall in the main entry hallway.

Nicholas County was initially created by an act of the Virginia General Assembly on January 30, 1818 from parts of Greenbrier, Kanawha and Randolph counties. The county's boundaries were disputed and altered to its current status by another act of the Assembly two years later. It is named for Wilson Cary Nicholas, Governor of Virginia, 1814-1816.

The first meeting of the Nicholas County court took place on April 7, 1818 at the home of John Hamilton, who donated 30 acres of land for the establishment of the county seat. The record of the meeting is still available in Book A in the County Clerk's office. The land donated by Hamilton was formally established as Summersville on January 19, 1820, and incorporated in 1897. It is named for Judge Lewis Summers, who was responsible for introducing the bill in the Virginia General Assembly to create the county.

Early court records show that Virginia law required that all officials take four oaths: the oath of fidelity; the oath to support the Constitution of the United States; the oath to suppress dueling; and the oath to faithfully discharge the duties of the particular office.

The early county court, under Virginia law, had almost unlimited jurisdiction, which included criminal cases and most civil actions. It appointed all the county officials, with the exception of the Circuit Clerk, delegates to the General Assembly, and the Overseers of the Poor, who were elected. The powers and responsibilities of the court were far more extensive than they are today.

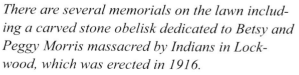

During one court session in 1818, the rates where fixed for tavern keepers in the county. *Breakfast – 25 cents; Dinner – 25 cents; Supper – 25 cents; Whiskey (one-half pint) – 12 ½ cents; Hay to horse (24 hours) – 21 cents; and Lodging – 12 ½ cents.*

There are several memorials on the lawn including a carved stone obelisk dedicated to Betsy and Peggy Morris massacred by Indians in Lockwood, which was erected in 1916.

In July 1861, 20-year old Confederate spy Nancy Hart led an attack on Summersville that resulted in most of it being burned. Later captured, she was held in the Summersville jail. She was given the privilege of walking in the jail's courtyard with a guard escort. One evening she asked her guard if she could examine his pistol. The guard, reportedly overcome by her beauty, gave her the weapon. She shot the guard and escaped. After the war, she returned, married, and remained in Nicholas County for the rest of her life

below: a park-style panel on the courthouse grounds tells the story of Nancy Hart.

The courtroom is modern, with dark wood paneling and wainscoting. Lighter wood accents provide contrast and detail. Stylized window treatments and a geometric design in the carpet add extra color to the courtroom.

The Nicholas County Courthouse was listed on the National Register of Historic Places in 1991. The county seat of Summersville is a gateway community to the Summersville Lake area and New River Gorge National Recreation Area.

below: a preserved, stamped metal panel from the old courtroom ceiling.

Nearly a block in length, this modern courthouse houses both city and county governments.

The January 30, 1960 dedication of the City-County Building was attended by 2500 citizens, Governor Cecil Underwood, Congressman Arch Moore, and every city and county elected and appointed officer. All attendees and speakers hailed the new courthouse as a *"modern bastion of democracy with all the accoutrements of the modern age."*

Ohio County Courthouse
Constructed ~ 1960
Style ~ Modern / Contemporary
County Seat ~ Wheeling

In 1776, the Commonwealth of Virginia established Ohio County, an area in excess of 1400 square miles, with the seat of government at West Liberty. There, at the place called Black's Cabin, the first judicial sessions were held on January 6, 1777. The following year "a diamond-cornered house of 22 by 18 feet [and]one story and one-half high" opened and remained the legal center for northwestern Virginia until 1797. *"West Liberty [was] a thriving town . . . with as many as many as 1500 to 2000 people,"* wrote one early visitor, commenting on the hustle and bustle of court days when residents came to town for legal business, to visit friends and taverns, to buy supplies, and to attend church. After Brooke County was created in 1797, the county seat moved to Wheeling.

In Wheeling, the first court session met in a private home, but in 1798, the county built a modest two story stone structure, located on 10th Street, between Main and Market Streets.

As Wheeling grew in population and economic importance in the first half of the 19th Century, residents expected a grander building in which to conduct their legal and civil responsibilities. On April 10, 1839, the cornerstone of a new courthouse was laid at the corner of Chapline and 12th Street.

view of the courthouse from 16th and Chapline.

In 1875, a new building on the corner of Chapline and 16th was constructed to house the state capitol. It served as the seat of state government until 1885, when the capitol returned to Charleston. The same year, the court and county offices moved to the former State Capitol. The courthouse was an example of Victorian eclecticism at its best; 60 different styles of architecture were employed in its construction. It was built to impress: ornate facades, a bell tower, a reddish stone exterior, and a massive presence. Its grandeur spoke to the important governmental functions within.

By the middle of the 1950s, voices for change rang out across town and across the county for change. The News Register called it a "poorly lighted fire hazard," and public opinion overwhelmingly supported razing the structure. In November 1955, voters in Wheeling and in the county approved the sale of bonds to finance construction of a new courthouse. A newspaperman summed up the dominant view: "Now hoary with age, outmoded and long since outgrown, with the bell tower about to collapse into the main corridors, the old building will be razed."

view of the north side of the courthouse showing the jail in the rear

Updated over the past half century, its communications center and offices are efficient and technologically current. One small feature which sets it apart from most other West Virginia courthouses is found near the Chapline Street entrance - a snack bar.

The Circuit Courtroom, while modest in size, is very efficient in its use of space. The modern courtroom is made more appealing with the extensive use of wood panels and trim

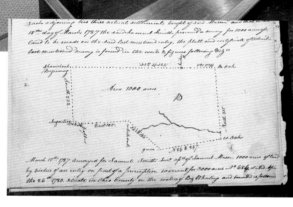

above: an old property map from 1787 - an example of typical, historic county records.

The courthouse houses both Ohio County government offices and those of the City of Wheeling. It is an efficient use of a public building and facilitates ease of communication between the different levels of government.

The entrance to city offices.

A snack bar is operated within the courthouse - a great convenience for employees and the public.

Located within the Franklin Historic District, the courthouse rises above the street level with its elevated foundation and steps up to the massive entrance portico which is supported by six Ionic columns. The stately courthouse is surrounded by a large, grassy lawn and a town square.

Pendleton County Courthouse
Constructed ~ 1925 / 1927
Style ~ Colonial Revival
County Seat ~ Franklin

Pendleton County was created by an act of the Virginia General Assembly on December 4, 1787 from parts Augusta, Harding and Rockingham counties, Virginia. It was named to honor Edmund Pendleton, a Virginia attorney and statesman. The first legitimate settlers in the county were six families who purchased 1,860 acres for a little over $230.00 in the town called Frankford. The initial meeting of the county court took place in June 1788, and one of the court's primary orders of business was to select a permanent county seat - they selected Frankford.

One of the first buildings constructed in the town was the county court house. It was made of logs and measured only 22 by 23 feet. It remained in service for 28 years before being replaced by a brick court house.

By 1794, the town population increased to around 50 citizens, which was sufficient to apply for a town charter. On December 19, 1794, the town was chartered by the Virginia General Assembly and the name changed to Franklin, due to another town in the state already called Frankford.

top right: artists' conception of the original courthouse;
above: the courthouse as it appeared in the 1930s

The current courthouse is the county's fourth; the previous courthouse was lost to fire in 1924. Constructed in the Colonial Revival style, the brick building has with a large central louvered belfry on the front and block modillions (brackets) in the front gable and roof eaves. The brick is accented with quoins and there is a stone water table. Citizens enter through the tall, two-story projecting portico centrally located on the front, which is supported by two-story tall Ionic columns and pilasters.

While much of the original integrity has been preserved, the south side of the building has been modified from the original porch configuration on the first floor to being infilled with brick to provide more interior space.

The interior is noteworthy for its fireproof concrete walls and floors, likely a result of the previous courthouse burning down. A mix of old and new can be found in the courtroom . The original railing, with wide spindles, and jury boxes remain. While the judge's bench and witness box do not appear to match the railing and jury boxes, they are equally attractive with smooth burled wood features.

A large hand-carved wood West Virginia seal is located on the wall behind the bench. A recent, 1995, renovation to the room installed lay-in ceiling panels, new oak wood benches in the gallery and hanging pendant light fixtures compliment the room.

On the courthouse grounds, a bronze World War I Memorial Marker sits at the front of the courthouse, next to the entrance. It lists the WWI veterans who were killed in action or died of wounds or disease. There is also a statue on a rubble stone pedestal of a Confederate soldier on the southeast corner of the lot.

The original York Safe Company vault doors are still used on the County Clerk's and Circuit Clerk's offices.

The courtroom is spacious and seemingly simple. However, there is a host of interesting detail. The railing is heavy and attractively old school. There is a raised alcove behind the judges bench.

Sitting on a high knoll at the edge of St. Marys, the Pleasants County Courthouse is approached by Court Lane, a long, stately, tree-lined drive. Visitors pass a well-maintained, center terrace divider with tall lamp posts adding to the landscape.

The courthouse is a simple, two-story brick building, constructed with elements of the Neoclassical Revival style.

Pleasants County Courthouse
Constructed ~ 1924
Style ~ Neoclassical Revival
County Seat ~ St. Marys

ST. MARY'S,
WEST VIRGINIA
1899.

Efforts to form a new county from remote portions of Tyler, Wood, and Ritchie counties began in 1847. The citizens' meetings that were held to organize the county were held in Alexander Creel's home.

The citizens voted for the project on April 27, 1848. Final success came in the 1850-51 session of the General Assembly, which approved the new county. It took a long time to fully organize the county and to establish public buildings. Because the population of the county was so small (1,500) at the time of founding, the county founders encountered much difficulty in raising the finds needed to build a courthouse and jail. Further, finding revenues to pay the modest salaries of the new county employees proved almost insurmountable.

above: an aerial view of St. Mary's in 1899. left: a view of the same showing the school (left) and the courthouse (right).

A committee of citizens designed the first courthouse and where tasked to find a suitable site for the construction. They accepted a parcel of land deeded to the county court in 1851 by Creel, the founding settler of the town. His deed stipulated that if the courthouse site ever changed, then his estate should be reimbursed only for the cost of the "naked" lot, and no subsequent improvements to the site.

The building the committee designed a Classical Revival building constructed of brick, at a cost of $5,300. They were contracted to build a combined courthouse and jail, with the jail in the basement of the building. Given one year to construct the building, they took until June 11, 1854 to complete the project. While the construction was under way, the court met at a private home.

The first courthouse featured a gable front entry, pedimented portico over a central entry, and a very tall belfry. It was constructed of locally fired brick. This courthouse served the county until 1919 when the automobiles became more popular and post-war prosperity triggered a desire for a newer, larger courthouse. That year, responding to a petition by citizens, a bond issue was put to a vote for a new courthouse that would be used to honor the county's returning war veterans: each of their names would be inscribed on the building, but the effort was not successful.

132

The county had no choice. In 1923, the courthouse cupola was struck by lightning causing a fire that badly damaged the building. During the construction, county offices were housed in downtown office buildings, a feature that was immediately popular with the citizenry because it was so convenient for them.

The site was on top of a steep hill, and was somewhat difficult to reach. In order to make access to the courthouse somewhat easier, the court purchased some additional land to the east, and on either side of the road up the hill, extending the court square. This acquisition allowed for the construction of a courthouse, a jail, and a jailer's residence, closely located behind the courthouse proper. Parking for automobiles was also included in the design.

The front portico rises the full two stories. It is reached by a wide set of sandstone steps. The pedimented portico and its entablature are supported by four tapering fluted Doric columns. The entablature on the pediment bears the inscription "Pleasants County Courthouse." This entrance has original double-doors, multi-light side lights and transom.

All of the window openings have brick lintels and sills. Above the doors is a flat cornice supported by decorative scrolled brackets.

Two stringer courses of brick near the parapet of the building frame a decorative course of vertical brick, comprising the only detailing on the building's exterior.

The courtroom is detailed with oak wood trim, flooring, and furnishings. Gallery seating is also of oak, in the form of theater style seating placed at a slight angle facing the center of the courtroom. The original size of the courtroom has been reduced in the rear to provide additional office space.

The Pocahontas County Courthouse is located on a full city block on the southern edge of Marlinton, the county seat. The large, courthouse square is slightly higher in elevation than the remainder of the downtown, giving the center of government a prominent location within the community.

A brick addition, visible to the right in the above picture, was completed in 1976. Consisting of a one-story rear section, it wraps slightly around the sides, covering the two south, first floor bays. Its impact on the historic visual characteristics of the courthouse are minimal due to its location and overall scale.

Pocahontas County Courthouse
Constructed ~ 1893 / 1895
Style ~ Romanesque Revival
County Seat ~ Marlinton

Pocahontas County was created by an Act of the Virginia General Assembly on December 21, 1821. The land came mainly from Bath County, with small tracts of Randolph and Pendleton counties. The first meeting of court was held on March 5, 1822, at a private home near Huntersville.

Huntersville served as the county seat until 1891, when the county's residents voted to move the seat to Marlinton. The move was prompted by transportation and industrial development. Marlinton, known as Marlin's Bottom until 1887, had few residents. Colonel John McGraw, of Grafton, through the Pocahontas Development Company, offered $5,000 for the construction of a new courthouse, if the county seat was moved to Marlinton. They subsequently also paid for, and provided the temporary courthouse during the construction years.

The voters approved the the relocation of the county seat on December 8, 1891. The struggle with Huntersville did not die immediately, and a second vote was authorized in 1894. Again, the voters chose Marlinton. From a newspaper account of the day:"*It would take more money and whiskey to get it (the court house) back to Huntersville than it did to move it to Marlinton.*"

The Pocahontas County courthouse is a stately, two-story building. The central block has a steep hip roof and on the front elevation with with a broad arch over the entrance door. Above the arch is a simple wood entablature supported by corbeled stones. The arch and entablature are supported by doric columns of stone. Above each pair of first-floor windows is a cartouche panel of stone. The east one has carved "POCAHONTAS; the west one "COURT HOUSE.

High, arched windows are plentiful and provide ample light to rooms and hallways, making the interior bright and inviting.

The interior of the first floor of the courthouse consists of a central corridor with stairs to the second floor in the intersection. The hallway is exceptionally wide - offering easy access to county offices. The major, original feature of the interior is the vertical board, hardwood wainscoting in all rooms. The entrance doors to the vestibule are paired hardwood .

A striking feature of the interior is the hardwood stair and balustrade in the main staircase. The newel posts are square with chamfered edges between the base and the top rail section. They have applied round bullseye ornaments in the panels. They also have a ball finial. The balustrade consists of turned baluster with square caps and bases that support an intermediate rail. This rail supports turned blocks that support the main rail.

The court room which occupies the majority of the second floor. The judge's bench and jury box are not original, but the main rail and the public seats date from the construction of the building. The seats are bent wood with shared wood arms. The ends of each row have decoratively painted panels.

left: a memorial to Pocahontas county veterans is located on the grounds.

right: the spacious and attractive jury room.

The Preston County Courthouse is located on a prominent corner in Kingwood's downtown and surrounded with a large, grassy lawn. The current courthouse is the fourth to be built in the county seat.

The lawn of the courthouse contains a cannon that was fired in defense of Fort Sumter in April 1861. It is a Columbian Siege Gun, twelve feet long, with an 8-inch bore and weighs 8500 pounds. The cannon was dedicated on July 31, 1912.

A bronze plaque near the entrance identifies the building. It also draws attention to the intricately grained sandstone exterior.

Preston County Courthouse
Constructed ~ 1933 / 1934
Style ~ Art Deco
County Seat ~ Kingwood

What is now Preston County was first settled in c. 1752 by brothers, Samuel, Gabriel and Israel Eckerlin (or Eckarly), who were members of the Dunkards, an offshoot of the German Baptist Church. There are conflicting accounts of the fate of the brothers during the French and Indian War. It is believed that Gabriel and Israel were captured and Samuel eventually returned to the Philadelphia area. By 1790, there were approximately 1,000 people living in the county. During the 1790s, John Miller and Hugh Morgan owned the land that would later become Kingwood. The exact date the town was laid out is not known because a fire at the Monongalia County courthouse in 1796 destroyed the county's records.

The Virginia General Assembly established the town by legislative enactment on January 23, 1811. Kingwood was incorporated by the Virginia General Assembly on March 22, 1853.

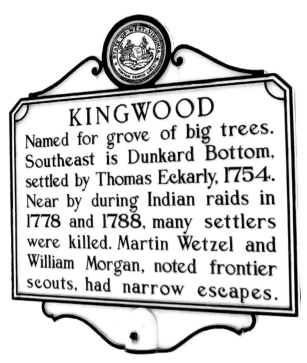

KINGWOOD
Named for grove of big trees. Southeast is Dunkard Bottom, settled by Thomas Eckarly, 1754. Near by during Indian raids in 1778 and 1788, many settlers were killed. Martin Wetzel and William Morgan, noted frontier scouts, had narrow escapes.

The county was formally created by an act of the Virginia General Assembly on January 19, 1818 from parts of Monongalia County. It was named for James Patton Preston, Governor of Virginia (1816 - 1819).

left: a portrait of Governor Preston hangs in Circuit Courtroom.

The first meeting of the county court was held in early April 1818 in the house (tavern) of Colonel William Price in Kingwood. The house was known for years as "Herndon Hotel." During the first meeting, it was decided to purchase a store, owned by a John S. Roberts, to serve as the county courthouse. It was used for court trials beginning that first year of the county's formation.

Court House and Soldiers Monument, Kingwood, W. Va.

left: a photo of the 1870 courthouse.

below: an architect's drawing of a proposed design for a new courthouse in the 1930s.

A stone courthouse was built about 1821 on the site of the present courthouse. The next courthouse was finished in 1857 and destroyed by fire on Sunday morning, March 7, 1869. The county rebuilt in 1870 and that courthouse was torn down in 1932. Two years later, the present courthouse was opened.

The current Preston County Courthouse was dedicated August 25, 1934. The final cost of the building was $113,500.90. It is a two-story, Art Deco style building with a striated yellow sandstone facade. The building is rectangular and has a flat roof, with a raised basement and facade which is divided by pilasters that project above the roofline. It is one of the few Art Deco style courthouses in the state. Art Deco designs became popular internationally and flourished in the 1930s and 40s. The style is marked by rich colors and bold, geometric shapes.

A memorial to those who served in the Civil War is also located on the courthouse lawn. The monument is granite and thirty-five feet tall. The statue was designed to represent the Civil War soldier from Preston County. Begun in 1895 and completed in 1903, the inscription reads: "*In Memory of the Soldiers and Sailors of Preston County 1861-1865.*" Unveiled on October 31, 1903, newspaper accounts state that it was a beautiful day and more than 5000 people were in Kingwood for the event, including 100 Civil War veterans.

The large courtroom is a combination of the modern and traditional. Red carpeting and draperies add a bright color element to the dark tones of the wood.

The floors of the entryway and stairs are a mosaic of native stone, creating very colorful and practical walkways in the building.

Many courthouses have a clock. Preston County is no exception, only in this case it stands independent of the building. It is colorful and beautifully ornate in design, adding a unique element to the courthouse grounds.

Facing northwest toward the town of Winfield, the Putnam County Courthouse stands at the edge of a terrace above the Kanawha River. Mature hardwood trees grow around the building on a well-kept gassy lawn. A gradually sloping stairway provides access to the front entrance of the seat of county government.

Putnam County Courthouse
Constructed ~ 1900
Style ~ Romanesque Revival
County Seat ~ Winfield

Putnam County came into existence on March 11, 1848 by an act of the General Assembly of Virginia. Created from parts of Kanawha, Mason, and Cabell counties, it was unnamed at the time. After county offices were organized and officials in place, the county took the name of Revolutionary War General, Israel Putnam. County trustees named the county seat after General Winfield Scott, who became a national figure following his success in the Mexican-American War.

The new county government found temporary lodgings on the banks of the Kanawha River in a private residence. Elected officials, tasked with building a permanent courthouse, purchased land, and after raising $4,000.00, secured contractors to build a brick courthouse in 1848.

With its location on the Kanawha River, Winfield, quickly became an active and growing community as a steamboat port as well as county seat. By the late 1890s, county officials began plans to replace the courthouse. The final decision for new construction came following the courthouse's collapse during a windstorm in September, 1899.

With the courthouse declared "*unfit for use and occupancy as a courthouse*" the county court moved to a local Baptist Church, paying $2.50 per month in rent. The county took possession of its new courthouse on September 16, 1900. The cost for the construction was $14,713.31, which included $1,075 for the installation of a steam heating system.

While the courthouse is obscured much of the year by foliage, taking the opportunity to view the architecture is well worth the time. The original structure of the Romanesque Revival-style building is a two story rectangular block with a hip roof and four octagonal towers, one at each corner. Each of the towers have an eight-sided conical roof. A clock is located in the west tower, which is taller than the others. The walls are laid in common bond brick with several areas of texture, patterns, and corbeling present for visual relief. The building is generally oriented with its corners pointing in the cardinal directions.

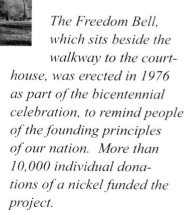

The Freedom Bell, which sits beside the walkway to the courthouse, was erected in 1976 as part of the bicentennial celebration, to remind people of the founding principles of our nation. More than 10,000 individual donations of a nickel funded the project.

In 2000, the 52,000 square foot Putnam County Judicial Center was completed in response to the changing physical and security needs of the circuit court system.

The interior of the courthouse, as with many, has been modernized while retaining original elements. The spiral staircases in the front towers remain as does the second floor courtroom. Actual court proceedings take place in the Judicial Center.

Standing to the northeast of the courthouse is a WWI Doughboy statue. The life-sized figure has its head turned to portray the ceremonial drill position of "eyes left." Both hands hold a rifle by the barrel with its butt to the ground. Each of the four sides displays carvings symbolizing each branch of the military.

Near the front entrance stands a memorial to all the first responders who dedicated themselves to the safety of Putnam County citizens

A sword and plowshare are combined in a monument dedicated in 1991 to MIAs, POWs, and KIAs. It was provided by Boilermakers Union #667, Winfield.

Hanging above the entrance is a small bell that originally belonged to the Kanawha River steamboat Blue Ridge. After the Blue Ridge exploded and sank in 1848, the bell was salvaged and used for the first county courthouse, which was under construction at the time. Following the collapse of the first courthouse in 1899, the bell was pulled from the wreckage and hung from the portico of the new courthouse, where it remains today.

The Raleigh County Courthouse is located in downtown Beckley on a large level lot, surrounded with a grassy lawn and trees. Since it was determined the previous courthouse was inadequate to meet the growing needs of the county, a new building was constructed, becoming the third courthouse at this location.

A memorial to all veterans is located on the left of the building

Attached to the front of the courthouse, is a bronze plaque - a reminder that the courthouse was occupied by Union forces during the Civil War.

Raleigh County Courthouse
Constructed ~ 1936 / 1937
Style ~ Art Deco
County Seat ~ Beckley

Beckley was established on April 4, 1838 and known as Beckleyville at the time. General Alfred Beckley, one of the first settlers in the county, was responsible for both the county and town's establishment. He was also largely responsible for the construction of the Giles, Fayette and Kanawha Turnpike which opened a route from Virginia to Kanawha County.

Raleigh County was founded on January 23, 1850 from parts of Fayette County and named for Sir Walter Raleigh, in honor of his early efforts to colonize Virginia for England. The first court convened in March of that same year. In addition to conducting court trials, the County Court had administrative duties, which included appointing the county board of education, laying the school levy, selecting the overseers of the poor, a county coroner and county constables.

The public school building was used until a courthouse was completed in 1852. Records show that for the first courthouse "*two large stoves not to exceed $46.00 were to be purchased for the courtroom.*" The cost of the brick courthouse was $2,722.00.

Two acres, for a public square and the site for the courthouse, was donated to the county by Alfred Beckley. He also provided, at no charge, the use of his timber and sawmill for the first courthouse. The following year, he sold 21 lots to the County Court for the sum of $1.00. The county could then sell the lots to raise the needed funds for the construction of public buildings.

Construction on this courthouse was reported as inadequate and in 1855, courthouse records were moved to a Baptist Church in the town. In the July 1856 term, the court "*ordered that Mrs. Minerva Haden be allowed one dollar.... for the use of her school room on this day to hold this term of court.*" Court sessions moved for four years until the courthouse was accepted for use by the County Court.

The second courthouse as it appeared on a postcard in 1920.

Growth to the town was slow and was referred to as "*Beckley's Paper Town.*" The first business was not established until 1850. By 1860, the town's population had grow to only 160, with another 160 living in the vicinity. The name "Beckley" came into use in the late 1890s, and the town was incorporated by the West Virginia state legislature on April 26, 1927. As the coal industry began to grow, so did the county. In 1893, the second courthouse was completed, at a cost of $34,354. It was used until 1935.

A time capsule is located on the side of the obelisk at the right of the courthouse.

The present courthouse is a two-story, Art Deco style building constructed of Indiana limestone. The majority of the funding for the project came through the Works Progress Administration (WPA). The windows are recessed and arranged vertically with metal spandrels between the first and second floors. The symbols within the recesses are representative of Roman authority, appropriate for a courthouse. The facade is divided into three sections and is eleven bays wide. The entrance

is rather simple with a stone surround and a small set of steps leading up to it. Engraved above the entrance door is the name, date and elevation information.

The Raleigh County Courthouse was listed as a contributing resource within the Beckley Courthouse Square Historic District on August 31, 1994. It is only one of three Art Deco style courthouses in the state; the others are Mercer and Preston County Courthouses.

In 2012, the Raleigh County Judicial Center was completed. The 70,000 square foot building houses the circuit, magistrate and family courts.

above: a second, smaller courtroom is available in the current courthouse. It is unique in design.

left: the main courtroom is quite large with wainscoting and detailed wood trim.

Sitting as a prominent feature of downtown Elkins. The native stone facade emphasizes the strength and mass of the building, and at the time of its completion, was a genuine statement about the power of industrial development in Elkins.

Randolph County Courthouse
Constructed ~ 1902 / 1906
Style ~ Richardsonian Romanesque
County Seat ~ Elkins

Randolph County was formed from Harrison County in 1787 and was named for Edmund Randolph, Governor of Virginia (1786 - 1788) and Attorney General and Secretary of State of the United States. It is the largest county in the state, even after losing part of its lands in the formation of Pocahontas, Barbour, Upshur, Tucker and Webster Counties. The county seat was established at Edmundton in 1787, which was later renamed Beverly, in honor of Virginia Governor Beverley Randolph (1788 - 1791), and chartered in 1790. Beverly, a small but thriving farm community, benefited greatly from the trade along the Staunton-Parkersburg Turnpike.

In June 1808, a committee was appointed to contract to build a brick courthouse to replace the original log structure. This building cost approximately $1200, including $35 for hinges and other ironwork. The courthouse was completed in 1815.

The 1808 court house is a two-story brick building, three bays by three bays, which originally had similar north and west facades and a bell tower on the roof. Today, it houses an exhibit describing the history of Beverly as the original county seat, as well as the 1890s courthouse feud between Beverly and the burgeoning city of Elkins.

The courthouse in Beverly.

In 1889, Stephen B. Elkins and Henry Gassaway Davis built the West Virginia Central and Pittsburgh Railroad into the Tygarts Valley to develop the area's timber and coal resources. By 1890, the new town of Elkins was incorporated. Bearing the name of its founder, it was located just seven miles north of Beverly. With the coming of the railroad, Elkins eclipsed Beverly in size and wealth. This shift in economic power triggered a struggle for political control and the location of the county seat. The issue was put up to a public vote, with the first victory to Beverly. However, the dissatisfied residents of Elkins quickly complained that the courthouse in Beverly was too small. A new courthouse was constructed in 1894, but it stood for only three years. The ill-fated courthouse was destroyed by fire in 1897. Each side blaming the other for the blaze.

Randolph County Court House, Elkins, W. Va.

The dispute became so serious, that in May 1898, Beverly's sheriff deputized 100 citizens. Armed with rifles and dynamite, the defenders dug trenches around the courthouse to prepare for an impending assault from Elkins. The confrontation was averted at the last minute and in 1900, Elkins won the county seat.

Construction began in 1902 and was completed within four years at a cost of $110,281.00. Once completed, it was referred to as *"one of the most handsome, substantial, and conveniently arranged Temples of Justice in the state of West Virginia."*

above: the defenders of Beverly pose - armed and determined to repel an attack from Elkins.

The newly completed courthouse as it appeared in 1908.

A tall tower, 150 feet in height, is the most prominent feature and flanks the gabled entrance and rounded arch doorways. The detailed arched windows and doorways, that are accented with stone trim, add elegance to this outstanding architectural design.

Locally quarried stone was used for the construction. Transported on flat cars, the huge stones were hand cut by stone masons at the building site. A steam crane was used pick up the stones and place them.

At the second level of the exterior, to the left of the entrance, visitors will find a larger-than-life figure holding the scales of Justice

A richly detailed round tower, capped with the same copper roof, counters the larger central tower.

Much of the interior has been modernized. The second floor courtroom, with stained glass skylight, has been restored in recent years. The octagonal room seats 300 in the gallery.

The Ritchie County Courthouse, located in Harrisville, is high-style architecture. The Neoclassical Revival courthouse, with its two-story portico and clock tower, dominates the seat of county government.

Ritchie County Courthouse

Constructed ~ 1923
Style ~ Neoclassical Revival
County Seat ~ Harrisville

Settlement of the area that became Ritchie County began in 1800 as farmers settled in the area that became the town of Pennsboro, followed by property around Harrisville in 1803. The town of Harrisville, originally named Solus, was established in 1822 on property owned by Thomas Harris, with the intent it would become the county seat when a new county was formed.

In 1832, the Virginia State Assembly adjusted the state land laws. This encouraged more settlement in remote areas. Combined with the construction in 1830-40 of the Northwestern Turnpike (now U.S. 50), Ritchie County became a desirable place to settle. A few years later, the Staunton-Parkersburg Turnpike (SR 47) was built through the southern section of the county. The county's population doubled by 1850, and had nearly doubled again 10 years later.

above: the original brick courthouse and annex.

Ritchie County was formed in 1843 by an act of the Virginia legislature from portions of Lewis, Wood, and Harrison counties. It was named after Thomas Ritchie, editor of *The Richmond Enquirer.*

The first meeting of the Ritchie County Court was held in a private home on April 4, 1843. The Methodist Episcopal Church was rented as a meeting place while a site for the courthouse was acquired. By summer, a lot for a courthouse was deeded to the county. The first permanent courthouse was completed in 1874. It was built of brick and needed an annex by 1899 to house the circuit clerk, county courtroom, and county clerk's office. Eventually, the county bar petitioned the county court for a courthouse that was more suitable for a seat of law and on May 30, 1923, the present building's cornerstone was laid.

The portico is supported by four fluted, Corinthian columns. The pediment is decorated with dentil moulding and a shield featuring a stylized "R" resting on acanthus leaves.

The tower features an octagonal domed roof with a cupola, arched molding at the edge, and pilasters on each of four faces. Urn finials and louvers accent the lower tower walls.

The interior is as striking at the exterior. The center rotunda is accented by white plaster pilasters with Doric capitals, the floor is terrazzo with a star and compass motif, and sandstone wainscoting lines the halls.

The stairs leading to the second floor courtroom have the original decorative railings. The double entry to the expansive courtroom is topped by a diamond-pane transom and a broken pedimented arch above a wide wooden entablature.

The bench, also of oak, is framed by two pairs of massive fluted pilasters supporting a flat arch above. The conference room door directly behind the bench is trimmed with an ornate flat arch. Flanking doors to offices and the jury room are trimmed with curved arches. Oak spindle railing encloses the jury box and seating as well as separating the gallery from the court.

Theater-style seating is in the gallery and balcony. A domed ceiling, which features a skylight provides natural light to the room. The courtroom can seat at least 350.

The balcony and floor seating have a slight curve in keeping with a theater-style design, which focuses attention on the center of the courtroom.

The Roane County Courthouse sits on a level ground on the north side of Main Street. It is the third courthouse in Spencer located on the same site. Both previous courthouses were lost to fire and unfortunately, records were destroyed. The present courthouse was built in 1964-65 at a cost of $600,000.

Roane County Courthouse
Constructed ~ 1964 / 1965
Style ~ Modern / Contemporary
County Seat ~ Spencer

Present-day Roane County was explored by Albert Gallatin in 1785. He claimed over 50,000 acres of land in the area, including present-day Spencer. Indian hostilities and the lack of transportation in the area prevented its development and Gallatin turned his attention to politics. He later served as Thomas Jefferson's Secretary of the Treasury.

SPENCER
Visited, 1771, by Jesse Hughes, Indian fighter and scout. In 1812, named Tanner's Cross Roads for Samuel Tanner. To the west on the Marcellus Hart farm is the deepest oil or gas well east of the Mississippi River. 9104 feet.

Roane County was created from parts of Gilmer, Jackson, and Kanawha counties on March 11, 1856 and named in honor of Judge Spencer Roane, a Virginia attorney and statesman. Spencer was known earlier as Tanner's Cross Road, Cassville and New California before becoming known as Spencer in 1858.

Local history tells that Samuel Tanner and his wife, Sudna, were Spencer's first residents, arriving in 1812. The Tanner's daughter, Elizabeth, was born that year, reportedly while they lived in a cave. In 1849, Raleigh Butcher, who had planned to travel to California in search of gold, stopped in Cassville and stayed. He opened a popular tavern and the area became known as New California.

Court House, Spencer, W. Va.

The first meeting of the Roane County court was held in a private home on April 7, 1856 and the county's voters selected New California as the county seat. In 1858, the town was chartered by the Virginia General Assembly and renamed Spencer. The town was incorporated in the state of West Virginia on February 20, 1867.

left: the courthouse from 1915.

A monument, located near the left front of the courthouse, is dedicated to Colonel Ruby G. Bradley, the most decorated woman in the history of the US Army to date. A Spencer native, she was captured while serving in the Philippines during World War II. In a POW camp for three years, she stole food and medical supplies for other

POWs. She also served in the Korean War as a frontline nurse. Bradley retired in 1963 from the military and lived to the age of 94. She is buried in Arlington Cemetery.

The large interior illustrates its modern origins but complements the past through its use of marble wainscoting and terrazzo flooring. Stainless steel railings and pickets highlight the staircases that lead to the large courtroom.

A second monument is dedicated to the Battle of Spencer during the Civil War. Also on the courthouse lawn is the bell from the previous historic courthouse.

The two-story, flat roofed courthouse design is an interpretation of the Modernistic style, which was popular in the 1960s. The facade is brownish-gray brick and has a shallow portico formed by slender, smooth piers faced with white marble. There is no ornamentation except a gold mesh and filigree screen with a central state seal sculpture in cast aluminum located above the central entrance.

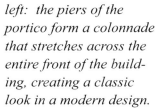

left: the piers of the portico form a colonnade that stretches across the entire front of the building, creating a classic look in a modern design.

above: below "Roane County" are three flags that announce that the county is home to the Black Walnut Festival - held in October each year and drawing thousands of visitors to the county.

The courtroom is finished in wood with a large black granite frontispiece behind the judge's bench. It is adoned with a silver eagle and the inscription, "Equal Justice Under Law."

The Summers County Courthouse at Hinton is known for its towers, which create a medieval castle-like appearance. The six, nearly identical towers, are octagonal in shape and were designed with ornamental brickwork of the tower eaves and open-brick, fretwork at the tower planes.

Summers County Courthouse
Constructed ~ 1875 / 1876
Style ~ Romanesque Revival
County Seat ~ Hinton

Summers County was formed in 1871 from parts of Fayette, Greenbrier and Monroe counties. The first County Commission met in an old, log Baptist Church at a location described as "*two miles up New River from Foss*". In 1872 the Commission moved into the upper floor of C.L. Tompson's Printing Office in Avis. In the following year, they moved to the storehouse near Hinton Island.

Hinton, which is located at the confluence of the Greenbrier and New Rivers, was incorporated in 1880. Hinton was built on land purchased by the Chesapeake & Ohio Railroad in 1871, from the son of the first white settler, Isaac Ballengee, who had received a Virginia land grant. The C&O linked the James and Ohio Rivers, and provided inland access from the eastern seaboard.

Prior to the C&O, only six families lived in the area, but after the railroad's arrival in the early 1870s, the population grew rapidly. The town was laid out in 1874 and hotels, taverns, mercantile stores, and boarding houses sprung up to accommodate the railroad workers. With the coming of the railroad, the C&O gave the county a site for a courthouse and in early in 1874, a $10,000 contract to build a courthouse was let by the County Commissioners.

A proposed design for the courthouse by architect, Frank Milburn.

The courthouse, when constructed in 1875-76, was a 48-foot square, two-story, brick building. Between 1893 and 1898, the original structure was rehabilitated and redesigned. Large octagonal towers were added to each corner and a slate roof was applied. Each tower contained about 400 square feet of space on both floors and they were connected on the interior to offices and the courtroom. A stairway was placed in the northwest tower, and a belfry capped the of the northeast tower.

Circa 1923, the courthouse space was increased by an addition with two towers at the rear of the building. During the 1930s, a flat-roofed addition was added to provide fire-safe rooms for county records and additional office space.

The towered parts of the courthouse were built of brick burned on the site and lumber from the nearby Hinton Island Mill. Local brick masons and carpenters were employed for the construction with the exception of the metal cornices and window pediments. The bricks were laid in courses of common bond, creating a very simple main building, but embellishments are found at window lintels and sills.

A view of the courthouse as it appeared on a postcard in 1910.

left: the ornamental brickwork and open-brick fretwork is clearly visible on the eaves and at the tower planes.

The courtroom is modern in appearance and layout. However, the exterior design of the towers is visible as angled corners in the courtroom. A small rope that was used to ring a tower bell to announce court, still hangs in one corner.

A special feature of the interior is the spiral, cast-iron stairway in the northwest tower, which extends to the second floor courtroom. The risers of the pie-shaped steps have a frieze with fleur-de-lis, a wooden rail tops the balustrade and the narrow banisters are joined together with iron scroll-work.

A monument to Confederate soldiers stands near the courthouse grounds. Interestingly, it includes a panel dedicated to the sacrifices of women during the Civil War.

Taylor County, named in honor of Senator John Taylor, a Revolutionary War soldier and Virginia statesman, was formed from sections of Barbour, Harrison and Marion counties on January 19, 1844.

Taylor County Courthouse
Constructed ~ 1880 / 1882
Style ~ Romanesque Revival
County Seat ~ Grafton

above: a view of the courthouse at Pruntytown.

During the mid-1770s, an area was settled in present-day Taylor County that became known as Cross Roads, due to its location at the intersection of the Washington Post Road and the Fairmont-Booths Ferry Pike. By 1801, Cross Roads consisted of ten cabins, a grist mill, a harness and saddle shop, and a blacksmith shop. The town was incorporated on January 1, 1801 as Williamsport, and was named the county seat when Taylor County was formed.

On January 23, 1845, the county seat's name was changed to Pruntytown. Early records show that in 848, Pruntytown's population reached 242, including 22 slaves. The town was evidently named for John and David Prunty, who had settled there circa 1798 and laid out the town.

The community continued to serve as county seat until 1878, when Grafton won the title in a special election. The change to Grafton was the result of the Baltimore & Ohio Railroad, which made Grafton a major railroad hub in 1852-53.

The current courthouse was constructed in 1880-1882 and the first in Grafton. The courthouse is a two-story, brown brick building in the midst of the downtown and lacks the traditional courthouse lawn or square. The original construction included a turret on the east corner and a tall tower on the west corner. Both have been removed, altering the original design.

above: the courthouse from a 1910 postcard.

The building is three bays wide, with the towers forming the end bays, and the center bay is the entrance, which consists of a tall one-story projecting end gable bay. The center bay is only two stories tall and is capped with a steep hip roof and a pedimented dormer. A statue of Justice originally sat atop the dormer further adding height to this vertical building, but it is no longer standing.

In the early 1920s, a two-story, hip roof addition on the west side with arched windows, brick corbelling and corner chimneys was added to complement the original building. This addition is two bays wide. In 1976 an annex was added.

Some historians claim that the town received its name from railroad crews who called it "graft-on" because several branch railroad lines met there. Other historians suggest that the town was named in honor of John Grafton, a civil engineer employed by Colonel Benjamin Latrobe, who laid out the route across what was then northwestern Virginia for the Baltimore and Ohio Railroad Company in 1852. Still others suggest that many of the area's settlers were Irish and named the town after their city of origin: Grafton, Ireland.

During the early 1840s, the Baltimore and Ohio Railroad company approached Monongalia County's political leaders about extending their rail line into the county. Fearing the railroad's effect on their way of life, they opposed the extension. Taylor County's political leaders welcomed the railroad. The B&O Railroad opened service to Grafton in 1853. At that time, 154 people lived in the town. The railroad's arrival led to an expansion of economic opportunities in the area, and Grafton's population began to grow.

Grafton was considered important by both sides during the Civil War, primarily because of the presence of the area's railroad lines. The Union Army maintained control over the town throughout the war. The only skirmish in Grafton took place on August 13, 1861 when 200 Confederate soldiers attempted to take the town. Twenty-one Confederate soldiers died during the battle but no Union casualties. Shortly after the war's conclusion, the Grafton National Cemetery was created. Completed in 1868, the Cemetery was to serve as a central burial place for West Virginians killed during the Civil War. During 1867 and 1868, 1,251 bodies of soldiers killed during the Civil War were exhumed from cemeteries throughout West Virginia and nearby states and reburied there. Private Thornsbury Bailey Brown, a member of the Grafton Guards, and the first Union soldier killed during the Civil War, was interred there in 1903. The National Cemetery is still active today. Grafton and Taylor County are also the birthplace of "Mother's Day."

above: the original courtroom in the present courthouse.

below: window restoration work.

The courtroom has been remodeled and modernized over the years. Today, it is spacious and bright. An interesting feature is that the jury box is located in front of the spectator seating, rather than to the side of the litigation well.

left: beautiful millwork accents the bench area.

The Tucker County Courthouse stands in the center of Parsons as a striking testimony to justice and county government. It is a fine example of late 19th-century public architecture in West Virginia.

Tucker County Courthouse
Constructed ~ 1898 / 1900
Style ~ Romanesque Revival
County Seat ~ Parsons

Tucker County was formed from Randolph County by an act of the Virginia General Assembly in March, 1856. In 1871, the West Virginia legislature added a small portion of Barbour County to its boundaries. The county was named for Henry St. George Tucker Sr. (1780-1848), a Virginia soldier, statesman and jurist.

The Virginia legislative act specified that the county court be held on the land on the east side of Cheat River. It was named St. George in honor of Henry Saint George Tucker, Jr., son of the county's namesake. The first session of the county court took place on May 22, 1856.

Fate would change the future of St. George. In 1888, a fire destroyed much of the town and the railroad by-passed it when constructing its line to present-day Elkins. The rail line led to the formation of Parsons, which by the mid-1890s eclipsed St. George in population. In 1889, and again in 1890, citizens of Parsons petitioned the county court to hold an election to relocate the county seat to their town. In 1890, the election was granted, but Parsons failed to obtain the necessary 60 percent majority vote to become the new county seat.

Elections were held again in 1892, yielding the same results. In the April 1893 election, the Parson's was successful in securing the county seat by a vote of 1,110 to 514. Leading citizens of St. George, claiming voting irregularities, asked the county court to overturn the election decision. The county court denied their request. St. George citizens then appealed to the state government, requesting an injunction on the county seat's relocation to Parsons.

Growing impatient, the citizens of Parsons organized a vigilante group of more than 200 armed men. On the evening of August 1, 1893, they went to St. George intent on stealing the courthouse records. The citizens of St. George gathered on the street leading to the courthouse, but fearing conflict, the Sheriff ordered the growing mob to disperse. When the Parsons' group arrived, most of the residents who had gathered by the courthouse were gone. They proceeded to break into the courthouse, and take the court records along with the bell from the courthouse's tower.

The Parson's group returned home and established a temporary courthouse in a nearly completed store on Main Street. The court continued to operate out of the store until 1900 when the current courthouse was constructed. The Parsons Advocate captured these words from a citizen of St. George: *"During the night of August 1, 1893, a group of prominent citizens and hoodlums from our neighboring town of Parsons zoomed into our thriving community with road wagons and on foot and literally stole our established county seat and moved it to Parsons ."*

The group that gathered in Parsons to seize the records in St. George.

Citizens posing as the county records are being moved into Parsons.

The current courthouse, the only to be built in Parsons, is of red brick, with stone banding, and accents of stone rustication. The striking edifice has a massive entrance portal of rock-faced stone and is flanked by two towers. The principal tower is four stories in height and capped with a steeply pitched roof. Each side has a clock face.

The courtroom is very traditional. Rich wood railing encloses the litigation well. A state seal hangs on the wall behind the bench. The walls and ceiling have been remodeled.

The seating is formed wood with cast iron framing. The courtroom boasts an original wood floor that is well maintained.

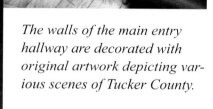

The walls of the main entry hallway are decorated with original artwork depicting various scenes of Tucker County.

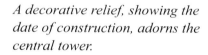

A decorative relief, showing the date of construction, adorns the central tower.

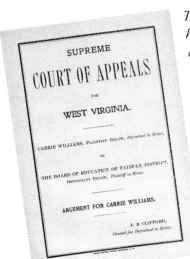

Tucker County was home to a landmark civil rights and education case more than 50 years before Brown v Board of Education reached the United States Supreme Court.

In 1893, John Robert (J.R.) Clifford, the first African-American admitted to the Bar in West Virginia, filed suit against the Tucker County Board of Education. The Board had reduced the school term of African-American schools from eight to five months. A black teacher, Carrie Williams continued teaching for the entire eight months, regardless of pay. The board refused to pay for the additional three months. Clifford argued against the decision to shorten the school year for African-American school children. Clifford won Williams v. Board of Education at a jury trial and was successful in 1898 before the West Virginia Supreme Court of Appeals.

The Tyler County Courthouse occupies a slightly elevated site in Middlebourne, the county seat. The courthouse we see today is a dramatic alteration of the 1854 courthouse, which is the core of this center of county government.

Tyler County Courthouse
Constructed ~ 1854
Style ~ Neoclassical Revival
County Seat ~ Middlebourne

Tyler County was created by an act of the Virginia General Assembly on December 16, 1814 from Ohio County. The county was named in honor of John Tyler, Governor of Virginia, 1808-1811.

Middlebourne, the current county seat, acquired its name because it was close to halfway between Pennsylvania and the old Salt Wells on the Kanawha River above Charleston. Established as a town by legislative action on January 27, 1813, it replaced Sistersville as the center of government two years later. The move was primarily due to Middlebourne's more central location and larger population (approximately 100).

A log jail was erected circa 1818, followed by the construction of an adjacent courthouse about 1820. In 1854, a two-story brick courthouse was completed. This building was transformed into the present courthouse in 1923, the year that electricity came to Middlebourne. The stone and brick for the new construction was transported on flat cars via street car lines from Sistersville.

The entrance of the courthouse is a pedimented two-story arcaded pavilion. Pilasters and balusters of limestone detail the brick arcade of the pavilion's second level. "Tyler County Court House" is located on the frieze and a relief of the pediment depicts Justitia, the lady of justice in mythology, sitting in judgment with the Sword of Justice in her left hand. She is flanked by a male and female who are seeking mercy.

left: a plaque pay tribute to the original courthouse (1852-1922)

right: There are several war memorials on the grounds. One is dedicated to the veterans of the Korean War.

The building has a copper-covered saucer-shaped dome, divided into three levels: a brick base, a louvered belfry, and a belvedere with clock faces.

left: a black granite obelisk stands in front of the courthouse as a memorial to the veterans of the Civil War from Tyler County.

The interior, while modified from the 1854 design, retains integrity of the early 20th century. The courtroom has a barrel vault ceiling with hanging lights that are suspended from molded plaster bases. It is a richly ornamented room. The center aisle slopes gradually to the front of the courtroom to the dais with its massive hardwood bench.

above: the judge's bench with a large, recessed arch, decorative pilasters, and dentil moulding.

HONOR ROLL
CITIZENS OF TYLER COUNTY
1917 — WORLD WAR NO. 1 — 1918
IN THE ARMED SERVICE OF OUR COUNTRY

GREGG, GARLIE	HORNER, FRANK	LIGHTNER, LAWRENCE	McCARNES, ALLEN H.
GREGG, LAYMAN	HOSKINSON, JEFF C.	LOGAN, CASEY	McCARNEY, ARTHUR
GREGG, LLOYD E.	HOSKINS, SILAS J.	LORAN, CASEY	McCARNEY, KHN
GRIMM, EARNEST O.	HOWARD, CLINT	LOW, ELIAS H.	McDOUGLE, CLARENCE
GRIMM, WILLIAM	HOWARD, FRANCIS L.	LOWE, ELI S.	McDUGLE, IVES
GROVE, WILBUR	HUBBARD, SAMUEL W.	LYTTON, HARRY	McELHOSE, EARNEST
GROVE, WILFORD G.	ICE, CHARLES	LYTTON, MYRON	McCOY, FRED J.
GUYTON, ORAN D.	ICE, DANIEL T.	MACY, G. D.	McCULLOUGH, ALBERT
HAMILTON, BRUCE M.	ICE, EVERETT	MAIN, DELBERT	McCULLOUGH, CHARLES A.
HAMILTON, EMERY W.	IRVIN, HARRY M.	MANNING, JOHN A.	McCULLOUGH, GEORGE B.
HANES, CECIL	JACOBS, DELBERT H.	MARSH, HARLEIGH H.	McINTYRE, BENTON
HANCART, STEPHAN	JOBES, EVERETT	MARSH, HARLEY	McINTYRE, CHARLES
HARD, WALLACE	JOBES, RALPH	MARSH, HARLEY T.	McINTYRE, CLARENCE
HARDMAN, BENJAMIN	JONES, BEN H.	MARSH, HERMAN H.	McINTYRE, LESLIE
HARLEMAN, LARSE P.	JONES, EDGAR H.	MARTIN, EARL	McINTYRE, LESLIE
HARPER, FRED H.	JONES, JESSE	MARTIN, ELI	McINTYRE, WILLIAM
HART, ALBERT	KELLER, ARCH L.	MARTIN, JAMES	NAY, CLAIRMONT
	KELLER, FREDERICK F.	MARTIN, RAY M.	NEFF, CHARLES

left: on the walls in the main entrance hallway are the Honor Rolls to the veterans of World War I and II.

The Upshur County Courthouse occupies a corner lot in the county seat of Buckhannon and serves as the entrance to the downtown area. The Upshur County Courthouse and Jail was listed on the National Register of Historic Places on December 31, 2009 as part of the Downtown Buckhannon Historic District.

The courthouse originally had a lawn area surrounding the building, but now sidewalks and streets front the building. In the remaining green space, there are three memorial plaques and markers on the courthouse lawn to war veterans.

Upshur County Courthouse
Constructed ~ 1899 / 1901
Style ~ Neoclassical Revival
County Seat ~ Buckhannon

An act of the Virginia General Assembly created the county on March 26, 1851 from portions of Barbour, Lewis and Randolph counties. The formation of the county was delayed as the neighboring counties objected to the loss of land from their own counties. It was named in honor of Abel Parker Upshur, a Virginia attorney and statesman, who served as President John Tyler's Secretary of the Navy, and Secretary of State.

On June 17, 1851, the first session of the county court was held at the home of Andrew Poundstone in Buckhannon. The town was officially incorporated May 1852. The county had a courthouse in 1854, which served the county until it was demolished in 1898.

above: the courthouse as it appeared in 1911.

The current courthouse is the second courthouse in town and its design is similar to the previous one in both the impressive entrance porticos and large octagonal domed cupolas. Some of the foundation stones from the previous courthouse were used in its construction.

The Neoclassical Revival style Upshur County Courthouse was constructed from 1899 to 1901 it a cost of $37,650. It is a simple red brick, two-story rectangle with a two-story high entrance portico. The portico is quite elaborate with dentiling in the entablature, and large, two-story tall Corinthian columns and pilasters flanking the entrance. A gabled pediment entrance is supported by Ionic columns and a large arched window. A painted stone surround with a central cartouche and the words "Upshur County" inscribed in the stone, and trumpeting cherubs or angels flanking the central cartouche, complete the entrance.

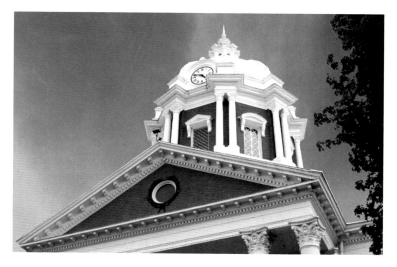

Above the portico is the very large octagonal cupola with clock and spire. The cupola has paired Corinthian pilasters with square-headed windows between them with heavy arched window hoods supported by end brackets and Roman grills. A primary cornice with symmetrically placed modillions and a large flat frieze resolve the exterior design.

The interior of the courthouse retains much of its original design, including the marble wainscoting and elaborate cove moulding at the ceiling level. As you enter the lobby, there are individual staircases to each side. The staircase railings are metal Roman grill panels topped with wood handrails and metal newel posts with ball finials. Newel posts at the bottom of each stair have etched torches with flames.

As with all courthouses, the courtroom is the most significant space in the courthouse. Renovated in 1970, the courtroom has a coffered, lay-in ceiling with every other square a light fixture. Wood panels, with peaked tops, cover the walls. Native wood, in dimensional panels, form the the judge's bench area, jury box, and separate the litigation well from the spectator seating.

below: an evening view of the illuminated courthouse which shows part of the annex in the lower left.

below: the courthouse appears as a silhouette during a lightning flash in 1910.

169

Wayne County was formed from a portion of Cabell County in 1842, and named for General "Mad" Anthony Wayne who fought the Native Americans for control of the region.

The courthouse is located on a prominent lot in the center of the town and is surrounded by a slightly elevated, grassy terrace. Large additions were added to the rear and sides of the original building in 1975 and 1976, which creates the impression that the original clock tower and belfry appear out of scale to the building.

Wayne County Courthouse
Constructed ~ 1922 / 1924
Style ~ Neoclassical Revival
County Seat ~ Wayne

The first meeting of the county court was held on April 11, 1842 at the home of Abraham Trout. Trout Hill was then established as the county seat, in honor of Trout, the first settler in the region and the owner of the land on which the town was laid out. The town was later incorporated on March 27, 1860 as Fairview. It was often called Wayne Court House by the local residents due to the presence of the courthouse. In 1911, the town's name was changed to Wayne.

Constructed from 1922-1924 at a cost of $110,000, the courthouse is a two-story brick and stone building with a central clock tower. The main block is three bays wide and each bay is defined by paired brick pilasters with a stone entablature above. The central double entrance doors have a simple stone surround. While the original window openings have been infilled with smaller window units, the original stone lintels and sills remain.

The county had several courthouses. The one that was in use during the during the Civil War, was occupied by troops from both sides. Local history tells that the large pine posts that were in the ceiling of the courthouse were hit with bullets then later covered with putty. After the war, older men would pick the putty out of the holes and take the bullets.

Wayne County also had a rival for the county seat. In the early 20th century, Kenova made a move to acquire the county seat, but in an election in Sept. 1921, the citizens of Kenova failed again to have the courthouse moved from Wayne to Kenova. Following the election, the citizens of Kenova were deciding whether or not to contest the election. The ballots were stored in the courthouse in Wayne waiting the final canvas. On Oct. 2, 1921 at approximately 3:30 a.m., a fire broke out in the courthouse. There was no firefighting equipment available but fortunately, the fire was contained to only part of the courthouse. Among the records lost were the 1921 tax assessment rolls and some of the ballots. The fire reportedly started in the south side of the building where the court room, circuit clerk's office and prosecutor's office were located.

A full view of the front facade clearly reveals the location and size of the original windows

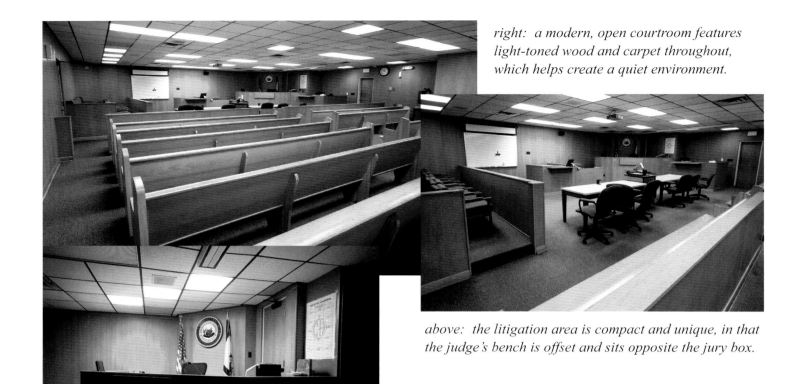

right: a modern, open courtroom features light-toned wood and carpet throughout, which helps create a quiet environment.

above: the litigation area is compact and unique, in that the judge's bench is offset and sits opposite the jury box.

above: the judge's bench in subdued lighting

below: both walls in the main entryway display photos honoring veterans. Some photos go back as far as the Spanish-American War. It also is an interesting historical exhibit.

below: on the front lawn is a World War I memorial with a sculpture of a "doughboy." Stone walls line the front of the courthouse lot at street level further defining the grounds.

On display on the grounds is an M5 anti-tank gun developed during World War II.

The courthouse is quite simple in style, but commands attention from its location on a tall knoll in the center of town, surrounded by a large grassy lot and tall mature trees. A small spring house remains on the courthouse lot as a reminder of the days when travelers came to the sulphur springs

WEBSTER SPRINGS
Originally known as Fork Lick for salt springs, known during Revolution, which attracted herds of game. Webster Springs was important health resort for many years. Town retains name of Addison for Addison McLaughlin, owner of its site.

Webster County Courthouse
Constructed ~ 1894
Style ~ Romanesque Revival
County Seat ~ Webster Springs

Webster County, named for the famous orator Daniel Webster, was the last county to be formed before the state's separation from Virginia. It was created from parts of Braxton, Nicholas and Randolph counties on January 10, 1860.

The county seat was incorporated in 1892 and has been known by a number of different names. It was first known as Fort Lick at Salt Springs; in 1892 it was incorporated as Addison; and eventually became known as Webster Springs for the name of the county as well as the sulphur springs. It has been known as Webster Springs since the 1930s but, the official name of incorporation is Addison..

A view of the courthouse as it appeared in 1909. Note that the connecting structure between the Sheriff's office and the Courthouse does not yet exist.

The current courthouse is the second courthouse to be located in the county seat. The first court was held in a private home prior to a frame courthouse being built. The frame building burned in 1888 and court was held in the Baptist Church until the current stone courthouse was built in 1894.

Construction cost for the courthouse was $11,900.00, a small amount even for the time period in which it was built. Upon first observation, the stone structure appears to lack architectural detail, but it has numerous elements of interest. It is a two-story, hip roof building with a central, short tower on the roof with a pyramidal roof. The facade is rough quarry-faced sandstone laid in regular courses. The main portion of the courthouse is three bays wide and the center entrance bay projects slightly with stone pilasters

with simple stone caps. The roof tower has round wood louvers and a plain wood cornice. The second floor windows all have fanlight transoms and arched stone hoods. The first floor windows are square-headed with rusticated stone lintels and sills.

The courthouse was designed by the firm of Franzheim and Giesey, who also designed the Fayette and Pocahontas County Courthouses and designed alterations to the Mineral County Courthouse.

A large stone side wing to the north houses the jail and sheriff's residence and office, effectively doubling the size of the courthouse building.

While the interior has had some modifications, the main entrance lobby retains its decorative colored vinyl tiles and original woodwork such as the paneled reveals in the doorways.

The large airy courtroom still has much of its original woodwork with paneled doors with transoms and corner blocks. The paneled oak judge's bench and witness stand are original as well.

A dropped ceiling has been installed in the courtroom, but even with that addition the ceilings are quite tall. The original plaster walls have been repaired and painted, and the spectator seating is oak benches with curved and scrolled end pieces.

left: the smaller, family courtroom is dedicated to judicial matters not involving the Circuit Court.

right: hanging on the wall of the Circuit Clerk's office is a reminder of one of the qualities in life that matters.

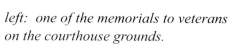

left: one of the memorials to veterans on the courthouse grounds.

below: the pavillion the marks the site of the "salt sulphur well" that was once so important in the community.

right: a large, single block of coal, mined in the 1930s, is a reminder of the importance of natural resources in the history of the county.

175

The county was named in honor of Lewis Wetzel, a frontiersman and guide who was born in 1764 on the South Branch of the Potomac River in present day West Virginia. His family relocated to the Ohio River Valley in 1769.

The facade above the portico is richly detailed with gable pediments and pilaster columns.

Wetzel County Courthouse
Constructed ~ 1902
Style ~ Richardsonian Romanesque
County Seat ~ New Martinsville

Presley Martin platted a town on his land in 1838 and named it Martinsville, after himself. It was named the county seat in 1846 as part of an act of the Virginia General Assembly establishing Wetzel County from the northern part of Tyler County, and was incorporated on March 18, 1848 as Martinsville. The town's name was officially changed to New Martinsville in 1871. The town's prefix, New, was added to distinguish itself from another town of the same name in Henry County, Virginia. The first meeting of the Wetzel County Court took place at the home of Sampson Thistle in April 1846, which was located on the corner of Main and Jefferson Streets.

In 1848, the ground now occupied by the courthouse was deeded to the county for the purpose of building a courthouse. The building was completed in 1852 and was in use until 1900. Early grand jury records indicate that nearly all indictments in the early years were for assault and battery, riding in a horse race on a public road or for selling bootleg liquor.

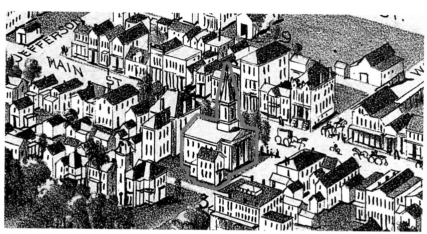

In 1902, the present courthouse was completed at a cost of less than $175,000. The courthouse style is considered Richardsonian Romanesque,

The courthouse in an 1899 drawing of New Martinsville.

which conveys elements from the architecture of Henry Hobson Richardson, who developed his style of design in the 1870s. The use of rugged stone and brick masonry was meant to present to the public a sense of solidity and stately presence. Since it was a combination of styles, courthouses, such was the one for Wetzel County, had a unique design.

S. Bruce Hall, the oldest member of the Wetzel County Bar Association, having served in the first courthouse, made this speech when presenting a gavel to newly elected James F. Shipman: *"The article which I am requested to present to you upon this occasion is an appropriate one. It is one of ancient and honorable use. It is the sincere hope of this speaker that you will not have occasion to use it frequently. We assure you that we have not selected this particular article by which to express our welcome for the reason that we think you are, or will ever become, a Knocker. This article carries sentiment with it. It brings back to fond memory, to some of us older members of the bar, the little old square courthouse, its large brick pillars in front, its squatty cupola, its high rostrum and sawdust floors of the courtroom, its stacks of old Army muskets, silent reminders of the carnage of former days, stowed away in an upstairs room, like the rusted toys of Little Boy Blue, of the hundreds of swallows who annually returned to build mud nests under its projecting eaves. I have no doubt, Sir, but what you will always live up to the highest ideals, and the finest traditions of the exalted office to which you have been elevated by voters of this circuit. Please accept this mallet from the Wetzel County Bar Association, in the spirit in which it is given. It is made from timber of our old Courthouse. Lift it with care, hammer with caution, and may it nor the Court ever fly off the handle!"*

On the grounds is a statue to Levi Morgan, a frontiersman (1736 - 1826). His grandfather was Colonel Morgan Morgan, who is credited for being the first white settler in what is now West Virginia. His father, Zackquill Morgan, settled present-day Morgantown.

The West Virginia Legislature of 1901 passed an act that appropriated $3500.00 for the erection of the monument. The monument was contracted through the West Virginia Monument Company, which was located in the county seat. On the 100th annniversary of the monument's dedication in 2002, the Weztzel County Chronicle reported that *"the monument company, not having a likeness of Levi Morgan, had a picture of "uncle" Aaron Morgan of Porters Falls taken. He was posed with one foot on a box and this was made to look like a stone when the statue was cut."*

At the rear of the courtroom is a large painting of Justicia - Lady Justice. She looks down upon the proceedings of the court as a reminder of the need for the legal system to be fair and impartial.

The courtroom is modern in design - open and spacious. A large portion of one wall is reserved for a collection of legal reference books - an in-house law library. The judge's bench is slightly offset and at the same level as the rest of the courtroom.

The Wirt County Courthouse is located in the small, rural community of Elizabeth, which borders the Little Kanawha River. The Neoclassical Revival-style building is central to a classic courthouse square.

One of two Civil War era cannons on the grounds, celebrates the Grand Army of the Republic, a significant veterans organization that existed from 1866 to 1956.

left: a memorial to veterans is located by the flag pole, in front of the courthouse.

Wirt County Courthouse
Constructed ~ 1911
Style ~ Neoclassical Revival
County Seat ~ Elizabeth

Wirt County was first settled in 1796 by William Beauchamp, who claimed 1,400 acres along the Little Kanawha River. In 1803 Beauchamp constructed a mill that spurred population growth in the area. By 1817 the area was formally laid out as a town. In 1822, the Assembly of Virginia incorporated the town of Elizabeth, which was named for Beauchamp's wife.

The county was formed January 19, 1848 from portions of Jackson and Wood counties. It was named for William Wirt, who served as a cabinet member of President James Madison. According to the West Virginia Historic Records Survey, the first courthouse was designed by Peter G. VanWinkle, who was paid $10 for his services. VanWinkle was an attorney, president of the Northwestern Virginia Railroad, a leader in the West Virginia statehood conventions, and served as one of the new state's first U.S. senators.

A new well spouts oil at Burning Springs.

In the mid-nineteenth century, the county's population increased greatly as industrialists came to nearby Burning Springs, which was found to be rich in oil in early 1861. More than 6,000 people descended on the town with dreams of the riches of an oil boom.

With the oil, came dramatic events of the Civil War. On May 9, 1863, General William E. Jones burned the oil drilling equipment in Burning Springs, along with the oil in the storage tanks. It is believed one hundred thousand barrels of oil were ignited and it was reported that the light from the fire was visible in the night sky as far as Parkersburg. The Confederates burned the courthouse in retaliation for a supposed Union burning of the Boone County Courthouse.

Prepared for the Confederate actions, County Clerk Daniel Wilkinson and his father, Dr. James A. Wilkinson, moved the county records from the courthouse, by horse and wagon, to safety in Parkersburg. Later in the war, Union soldiers used the shell of the original courthouse as a barracks.

The courthouse had to be replaced and the second courthouse served the county for approximately forty-five years before it was lost to fire in 1910. The county conducted business in Elizabeth's public school on Court Street as plans for a new courthouse were made. A new courthouse was completed in 1912.

A playbill for a production to be performed at the courthouse.

right:
the second courthouse that was destroyed by fire.

Civil War veterans gather for a reunion photo in front of the courthouse.

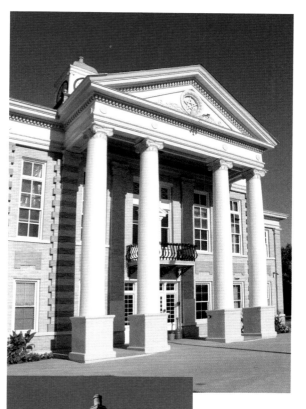

The courthouse is a two-and-one-half story brick building supported by a stone foundation. The main facade is dominated by a centered, full-height portico that is supported by four Ionic columns on brick bases and four Ionic pilasters. The dentiled cornice includes stone detailing above each column which is carried out around the building above each pilaster.

Directly above the main entrance is a small balcony supported by four decorative metal brackets and displaying a decorative metal balustrade. This balcony includes a center entrance with simple pilasters supporting a gable pediment.

Decorative brickwork separates the first and second story windows throughout the courthouse and decorative brick quoins provide ornamentation to the building.

A centered cupola has a wooden vent on each side, a decorative balustrade with corner finials, and a clock on each side.

The interior of the building features stairs with an original wood railing and newel post in the south corner of the building. Beyond the front entrance hall, the courthouse features a long central hallway with decorative terrazzo floor with dark oak trim and paneled doors leading to county offices located along each side.

The courtroom is located on the second floor. Decorated with oak railing, the room features rows of wooden benches on each side of the isle and an oak baluster separates the gallery from the court area. The judge's bench is raised in the center of the room and is also constructed of oak. Formerly, there was a balcony above the courtroom. The balcony was recently closed and is now used for storage.

right: an old watering trough, at the rear of the courthouse, is a reminder of the days when horses were a primary means of transportation.

The Wood County Courthouse has an imposing presence. Constructed over a two year period at a cost of nearly $100,000.00, it is massive in scope and has maintained its exterior architectural integrity for more than 100 years.

A fountain at the Market Street entrance features a bronze memorial to Circuit Judge James M. Jackson of Parkersburg. The memorial was erected in 1901.

Wood County Courthouse
Constructed ~ 1899 / 1901
Style ~ Richardsonian Romanesque
County Seat ~ Parkersburg

Wood County was established by the Virginia Assembly in 1798 from parts of Harrison County and named for the James Wood, Governor of Virginia (1796-1799). The settlement, then known as Newport, was made the county seat. In 1800, the Virginia Assembly granted a charter for Newport, on the north side of the Little Kanawha. Newport was rechartered and renamed for Captain Alexander Parker, who bought the property in 1785.

As with many counties, the first business of the court was carried out in a private home, and then as the county grew with the commerce that flourished on the Ohio and Little Kanawha Rivers, a two-story hewn log courthouse was built. The upper floor of which was used as the courthouse and the lower as the jail. The stocks, pillory and whipping post were reportedly nearby the jail. The courthouse was in use until 1817.

A drawing of the 1817 courthouse.

The second courthouse, built in 1817 at a cost of $25,000, was located on land donated to the county that today is known as Court Square. For its time, this courthouse was considered an elegant building, with a tall steeple and weather vane.

As the area continued to grow, it did not meet the needs of expanding government and was replaced in 1860 with a two-story courthouse that had Greek Revival columns and classical designs. This courthouse was also used by the city government until a city building was constructed in 1897. West Virginia's first governor, Arthur I. Boreman, was circuit judge and held court in the building from 1861 to 1863, and again from 1889 to 1896 following his term as governor.

Transportation was key to the growth of Parkersburg and the county. The Northwestern Turnpike was completed to Parkersburg in 1838 and the Staunton-Parkersburg Turnpike reached the county seat in 1847. The arrival of the Northwestern Virginia Railroad in 1857 provided an even greater link for river transportation to a growing population. Because of heavy lightning damage in 1885 and the continued prosperity resulting from the river, road and rail transportation, coupled with the region's oil and gas boom, it was determined the a larger courthouse was needed.

The image to the right shows the location of the present day courthouse, as it appeared in a cityscape from 1899. The Little Kanawha River is at the top, while the Ohio River is lower right.

183

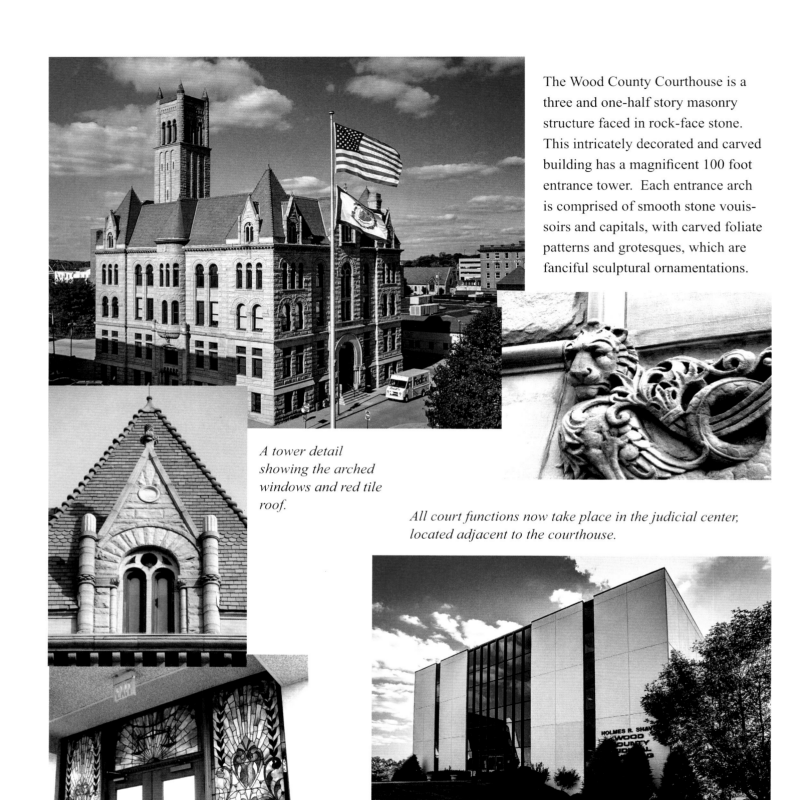

The Wood County Courthouse is a three and one-half story masonry structure faced in rock-face stone. This intricately decorated and carved building has a magnificent 100 foot entrance tower. Each entrance arch is comprised of smooth stone vouissoirs and capitals, with carved foliate patterns and grotesques, which are fanciful sculptural ornamentations.

A tower detail showing the arched windows and red tile roof.

All court functions now take place in the judicial center, located adjacent to the courthouse.

The interior of the courthouse has been remodeled but several outstanding elements remain. The iron stairwells and the stained glass sidelights to offices are original architectural features of the building.

The native, cut-stone, Wyoming County Courthouse is an excellent example of Neoclassical buildings of the early twentieth century. The massive fifty-four foot wide and twenty-four foot deep portico dominates the front elevation. A statue of the Rev. W.H.H. Cook stands in front of the courthouse. He served in both Confederate and Union armies, organized and taught the first free school in the county, and served in the state legislature.

There are multiple veteran memorials on the grounds. One marks the service of the first casualty of the Korean War.

On a lower terrace in front of the courthouse is a monument with five bronze medallions. Each represents a branch of the armed services. It is a memorial to all veterans who have served in all conflicts.

Wyoming County Courthouse
Constructed ~ 1916
Style ~ Neoclassical Revival
County Seat ~ Pineville

Wyoming County was formed from Logan County by Act of the General Assembly of Virginia on January 26, 1850. Oceana was the county seat from 1850-1906. In 1904, an election was held to determine the location of the county seat, and Pineville won. Those in support of Oceana appealed to the West Virginia Supreme Court and the election results were overturned. Pineville again won an election in 1905. In 1906, the West Virginia Supreme Court of Appeals ruled that Pineville would be the seat of county government for Wyoming County.

With the controversy settled, bond was given by eight men of Pineville, "*to furnish a suitable building for county purposes.*" The Thomas. A. Cook house was secured as the county's first courthouse. In 1909, the county bought several lots for a public square and constructed a temporary building with a stone vault. The issue of the county seat's location would rise again, with the town of Mullens making the case. An election was held in 1912, resulting in a decisive victory for Pineville with 1292 votes in the affirmative to 528 votes for locating the county seat in Mullens. In 1916, the present courthouse was built at a cost of $79,000.

Locally quarried and finished stone was used as the principal material construction material. The same material, dressed and smoothed, was used as quoins and as trim to accent windows and doors.

A striking feature of the Wyoming County Courthouse is the portico with triangular pediment. The portico is carried by four modified Roman Doric Columns. Matching these columns in size and height are four dressed limestone pilasters. The center block of the building is a gable with medium pitched roof while the wings have flat roofs with a balustrade that contain balusters in sets of four.

The former Wyoming County Jail stands beside the courthouse. It was built of the same native, rock-faced stone with some dressed stone used as trim. The three-story jail is ninety-four feet

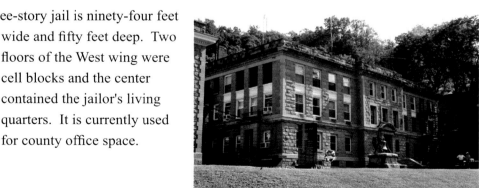

wide and fifty feet deep. Two floors of the West wing were cell blocks and the center contained the jailor's living quarters. It is currently used for county office space.

The building is surmounted by a small domed cupola with clock faces on all sides. Below the clock faces is a belfry with three open arches on each side.

The main entrance to the courthouse leads to a large, open lobby with coffered ceiling. From the lobby, citizens pass through hallways with arched entrances. Wood is used throughout in the solid doors and wainscoting.

The original integrity remains in all areas. On the first floor the windows are arched and transomed to match the entry, which has double doors and a draped fan light. The windows and exterior doorways of the building have dressed stone surrounds.

The second floor hallway provides access to the court-room.

below: the last citizen-ship ceremony held at the courthouse in 1954.

The stairways to the second-floor courtroom are open-well, three-flight, and with an open string. The string has ornamental brackets and the handrail is large and beautifully curved.

The courtroom is large with original solid, wood flooring. The litigation well is situated on a small riser, elevating it slightly above the main floor.

Elected County Officials

County government powers are separated among seven independently elected offices: the county commission, county clerk, circuit clerk (whose duties are with the circuit court system), county sheriff, county assessor, county prosecuting attorney, and county surveyor of the lands. Here is a brief look at the terms and primary functions of each of these offices.

The county commission is composed of three commissioners (Jefferson County is allowed five and Berkeley County has a 5 member council) elected on a countywide partisan ballot. Commissioners act as the county's legislative body and serve staggered, six-year terms. The main duties of the county commission are to determine the annual budget, submit a balanced budget to the state tax commissioner for approval, and set the county's levy rates on property. Commissioners also appoint a number of boards, and are typically involved in economic development work.

The county clerk is elected on a countywide partisan ballot to a six-year term. The clerk serves as custodian of all county records, and also is responsible for issuing licenses required by state government. This office also supervises all elections, with the exception of local municipal elections. Ohio County is the only exception - in this county the County Commission still oversees elections.

The circuit clerk, though an elected county official, is assigned to a circuit court, where he or she manages case filings and case records and collects court fees.

The county sheriff is elected to a four-year term on a county-wide partisan ballot. The sheriff is the only county elected officer who is subjected to term limitations. Formerly, the sheriff could serve only one term; a 1973 constitutional amendment allows for two consecutive terms. The sheriff's primary duties are to enforce the law and maintain order in the county. The sheriff is also the ex-officio county treasurer for both the county government and the local school district. The sheriff is an officer of the circuit court and any other court of record in the county, so he or she is responsible for serving papers, and summoning and impaneling juries. The sheriff is also the county jailer, serves as ex officio sealer of weights and measures, and appoints the county humane officer.

The county assessor is elected to a four-year term on a countywide partisan ballot. The assessor's primary duty is to appraise at full market value real estate and personal properties owned in the county. The assessor is also responsible for assessing and collecting a "head" tax on dogs.

The county prosecuting attorney is elected to a four-year term on a countywide partisan ballot. This is the only county officer not required to reside in the county he or she serves. The prosecutor's primary duty is to prosecute violators of the state's criminal laws. They also provide legal advice to the county commission and the county school district and represent the county in all civil actions.

The county surveyor of lands is also elected to a four-year term on a countywide partisan ballot. The surveyor conducts most of the county's land surveys, including those involving right-of-ways and alignments of roads and the sale or purchase of county lands.

"We in America do not have government by the majority. We have government by the majority who participate."

"Enlighten the people, generally, and tyranny and oppressions of body and mind will vanish like spirits at the dawn of day."

Thomas Jefferson

How To Rehabilitate A Courthouse

Michael Gioulis
Historic Preservation Consultant

An important ally in the process of rehabilitation is the National Park Service Technical Preservation Services. This is the arm of the National Park Service that is responsible for developing historic preservation policy, national standards and guidelines and educating the public and architects and professionals in the field of building preservation and rehabilitation. With over 150 publications, conferences, workshops, an extensive web site and other tools to assist stewards of historic properties, they are an invaluable resource. Perhaps one of the most valuable resources they offer are the Secretary of the Interior's Standards for the Treatment of Historic Properties. These are common sense principles in easy to understand language that guide the preservation philosophy of our nation. They are generally written, and as such, can be applied to almost any situation. All work on historic properties should follow the Standards, and, in fact, work that is undertaken using Federal funds or licenses must follow the Standards, according to the National Historic Preservation Act. Any work using Federal or West Virginia State funds must be reviewed by the State Historic Preservation Office to insure that it does not damage any historic character or resource. The reviews will follow the Secretary of the Interior's Standards.

The Standards are broadly written and are not technical prescriptive mandates. They are intended to provide a philosophical framework in which to make decisions about the preservation treatment, and provide a consistent direction to the work.

The first step in the process is to determine the level of action that will be undertaken. In most instances, what will be done is considered Rehabilitation. The attached sidebar is for clarification, but essentially, rehabilitation is the process of making a historic building useful for present and future needs. Acknowledging that some alterations may be necessary, completing the work in a manner that protects and preserves the significant historic features of the building is the goal. For example, in a rehabilitation it may be understood that it is necessary to install an elevator to allow access to various portions of the building. This is an allowable action, but it must be installed in a manner that does not damage historic materials, character or fabric.

Secretary of the Interior - Standards for Rehabilitation

The Standards are applied to projects in a reasonable manner, taking into consideration economic and technical feasibility.

1. A property shall be used for its historic purpose or be placed in a new use that requires minimal change to the defining characteristics of the building and its site and environment.
2. The historic character of a property shall be retained and preserved. The removal of historic materials or alteration of features and spaces that characterize a property shall be avoided.
3. Each property shall be recognized as a physical record of its time, place, and use. Changes that create a false sense of historical development, such as adding conjectural features or architectural elements from other buildings, shall not be undertaken.
4. Most properties change over time; those changes that have acquired historic significance in their own right shall be retained and preserved.
5. Distinctive features, finishes, and construction techniques or examples of craftsmanship that characterize a historic property shall be preserved.
6. Deteriorated historic features shall be repaired rather than replaced. Where the severity of deterioration requires replacement of a distinctive feature, the new feature shall match the old in design, color, texture, and other visual qualities and, where possible, materials. Replacement of missing features shall be substantiated by documentary, physical, or pictorial evidence.
7. Chemical or physical treatments, such as sandblasting, that cause damage to historic materials shall not be used. The surface cleaning of structures, if appropriate, shall be undertaken using the gentlest means possible.
8. Significant archeological resources affected by a project shall be protected and preserved. If such resources must be disturbed, mitigation measures shall be undertaken.
9. New additions, exterior alterations, or related new construction shall not destroy historic materials that characterize the property. The new work shall be differentiated from the old and shall be compatible with the massing, size, scale, and architectural features to protect the historic integrity of the property and its environment.
10. New additions and adjacent or related new construction shall be undertaken in such a manner that if removed in the future, the essential form and integrity of the historic property and its environment would be unimpaired.

Seldom will a project on a courthouse be considered a true restoration, though there may be limited instances and locations where this applies. It is often the case that a building can be separated into different areas of treatment, or zones.

These may be identified as: Restoration zone; Preservation zone; zones or spaces that have been so substantially changed outside the period of significance they no longer convey the historic setting of the building; or other identifications of levels of historic character. For example, the remaining original courtroom, with its detailed woodwork, bar, judge's bench, gallery, jury box, decorative elements such as molded plaster, stained glass domes, etc. may be considered a Restoration zone. Work done in that zone should follow the restoration standards and should be oriented towards returning the space to its original appearance, or to an appearance at a significant historical point in time. In the same courthouse, work in another area, such as the entrance lobby and corridor may be considered a Rehabilitation zone. Here the intent will be to preserve the remaining historic fabric, but allow installation of contemporary elements that make the building useful for continued functions, such as a new elevator, alternative doors and plan configurations etc. Finally, within the same building, areas may be designated as non-historic, due to their lack of integrity or historic features and their non-significance in relation to the history of the building. These spaces may be more readily altered as long as any remaining or discovered historic material is not damaged or lost. Thus, in a single building, there can be several different approaches to its preservation.

Meeting the Standards, however, is based on the cumulative effect of all of the work on the building, so care must be exercised in selecting treatments to specific areas of the building to insure the historic integrity is maintained.

> ### *Choosing an appropriate treatment for a historic building.*
>
> 1.   Preservation focuses on the maintenance and repair of existing historic materials and retention of a property's form as it has evolved over time.
> 2.   Rehabilitation acknowledges the need to alter or add to a historic property to meet continuing or changing uses while retaining the historic character.
> 3.   Restoration depicts a property at a particular period of time in its history, while removing evidence of other periods.
> 4.   Reconstruction re-creates vanished or non-surviving portions of a property for interpretive purposes.

The National Park Service also provides illustrated guidelines to assist in interpreting the Standards. From The Secretary of the Interior's Standards for the Treatment of Historic Properties with Guidelines for Preserving, Rehabilitating, Restoring and Reconstructing Historic Buildings:

According to the Sectretary of the Interior, "The Guidelines have been prepared to assist in applying the Standards to all project work; consequently, they are not meant to give case-specific advice or address exceptions or rare instances. Therefore, it is recommended that the advice of qualified historic preservation professionals be obtained early in the planning stage of the project. Such professionals may include architects, architectural historians, historians, historical engineers, archeologists, and others who have experience in working with historic buildings. The Guidelines pertain to both exterior and interior work on historic buildings of all sizes, materials, and types. "

Another critical resource that the National Park Service provides are the technical publications available. The most important of these are the Preservation Briefs. These are relatively short papers on specific topics relevant to historic preservation projects. They cover such topics as repointing mortar joints in historic masonry; improving energy efficiency; repair of historic wooden windows; preservation of historic concrete; repair of historic plaster; and making historic properties accessible. They are normally eight to twelve pages, with references and charts and photographs. There are currently 47 Briefs available. They are available online at the Technical Preservation Service web site: http://www.nps.gov/tps/how-to-preserve/briefs.htm.

Process: Identifying significant elements in the building

With the approach outlined above, it can be seen that a critical stage in the planning process is the identification and evaluation of significant elements in a building. All rehabilitation, restoration, maintenance and repair work should be undertaken with the knowledge of what is significant and how to protect it. Preservation Brief 18: Rehabilitating Interiors in Historic Buildings, and Preservation Brief 17: Architectural Character Identifying the Visual Aspects of Historic Buildings as an Aid to Preserving their Character, provide guidance on the approach.

A complete evaluation of the buildings elements is necessary to insure protection of the building's historic character. This includes researching the building's history, evaluating the extant (remaining) elements and assessing the changes that have occurred to the building. This will identify which elements of the building are considered historic. It may also include some elements that have been altered from original, but have gained significance in their own right and time period. Some evaluators categorize elements as primary and secondary depending on their importance in defining the historic character of the building. Primary elements are those that will require the most diligence in protecting and preserving them.

Primary spaces may consist of the more public spaces in the building and those that define and interpret the building's use. These can include spaces such as: the courtroom, the entrance lobby and corridors; large meeting spaces; monumental staircases; and gathering spaces such as rotundas. As can be seen, often the primary spaces are those that are more publicly oriented.

Secondary spaces are those that are generally associated with the more day to day workings of the courthouse. These are the offices, meeting rooms, reception areas, storage spaces, and workrooms. They are generally less detailed and ornate with fewer architectural details.

In addition to identifying the spaces, their condition must also be assessed to determine if they retain integrity. This relates to physical condition, damage and deterioration, alterations and retention of original or significant details and elements. Has the plaster ceiling trim been damaged by installation of a new dropped ceiling or heating equipment in the past? Does the large open space of a public meeting room retain its sense of space after subdivision into smaller offices? All of these questions will help identify which spaces and elements remain that may be considered significant and should be preserved. A combination of the historic significance of a space or element and its integrity will identify its position in the continuum of character defining elements.

A recent study of many of the courthouses in West Virginia resulted in the following partial list of identified significant or primary spaces and elements:

Finishes in the entrance lobby, terrazzo, wood stair details, metal ceiling, window trim and details.

Extant original doors, including decorative hardware.

Decorative vault doors.

Decorative pressed metal ceilings.

Corridor finishes including glazed terra cotta walls and terrazzo floors.

Architectural details in the courtroom and the furnishings, including the judges' bench, rails, jury box, etc.

Decorative stair details, including balustrade, rails and ornamental elements. These include all periods of architecture, such as Romanesque, cast iron newel posts and Art Deco marble walled balustrades with aluminum decorative rails and brackets.

Decorative plaster ceilings including cornices and molded ceiling sections.

Original counters in the Sheriff's office, County Clerks' Office and other public locations.

Murals in the building, often in the courtroom. These may have been commissioned by the WPA or date to an earlier period.

Memorial plaques and other furnishings and fixtures, such as mail boxes and chutes, water fountains, and light fixtures.

Case Study: Kanawha County Courthouse Exterior Restoration

Michael Gioulis
Historic Preservation Consultant

The Kanawha County Courthouse is an impressive Richardsonian Romanesque building in Charleston. Its character is defined by the heavy rusticated and rough faced stone exterior with arch details, carved columns and capitals and clay tile roof. A defining element in Romanesque Style buildings is the expanse and mass of the roof. Together with the heavy stone base, these create an appearance of solidity, grounded to the earth. It was these very elements that gave the building its identity that were in need of rehabilitation by the turn of the twenty-first century.

The original roof had been replaced in the 1980s with clay tile matching replacement. Unfortunately, by 2000 some of the tile had begun to deteriorate, sheathing was damaged, and sections of the roof had failed. There was also staining on the masonry from paint that had been applied to sections of the tile to match previously installed green tile to the red color of the roof. There was also failure of flashing details at the parapet caps and other roof intersections, failure of the ridge caps; failure at roof vents and skylights; and general deterioration of the roof.

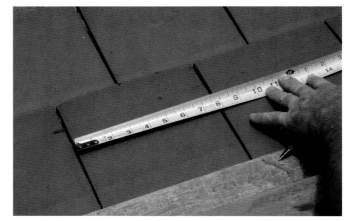
Measuring existing tiles.

The tile was a Ludowici French Interlocking Tile. The Ludowici Company has been in business since the 1800s. They became Ludowici-Celadon in 1906, and continue to manufacture clay tile in a variety of shapes and colors, often matching their historic patterns. Due to the significance of the building, and to the character defining status of the roof, the County Commission was intent on restoring the original roof appearance, rather than replacing it with a modern substitute or alternative material; having the original manufacturer still in business was a plus.

Gutters and downspouts were built-in design and many had failed or were in deteriorated condition. After extensive inspections and observations, to identify both the historic character of the tile and its defining details and elements, as well as patterns of deterioration and their causes, plans were developed to replace the roof, repair and replace any sheathing necessary; replace the flashing and all metal details and elements; and repair or replace other roof elements.

It was decided that the original tile would be used. This included the special shapes needed for details such as end caps, ridge caps and intersections. In addition, traditional installation methods would be used for the tile, copper nails. A tile roof is meant to be "hung" on the roof, rather than securely attached to it. Nails must be installed accurately to insure they

do not bind the tile to the roof too tightly, allowing it to move as necessary, and yet not allow it to move too much or fail. In addition, copper flashing was installed and regleted into the masonry. Copper gutters and downspouts were also replaced. Sheathing was replaced where it had deteriorated, to insure that the substrate or base of the roofing was sound and the installation would last as long as the tiles. A modern material was installed to insure water tight conditions at the perimeter of the roof and at critical locations, such as valleys and ridges. This material, a membrane ice and snow guard, was installed beneath the copper flashing as insurance in these critical areas. It is unseen when the roof is installed and meets the Standards, while providing additional protection. Other sections of the roof, which were flat portions and invisible from the ground, had been covered with a membrane roofing. This was replaced with a new membrane roofing.

All details were replaced on the roof to insure an appearance match. Some specific details of note include the eyebrow dormers on the east side of the building and the snow birds installed at the perimeter of the roof. The project was bid and the successful bidder was required to have a specialist in historic roofing on site to insure the quality of the installation. The end result is an historically correct roof, that functions properly and should last another one hundred years.

Water stains on the facade.

Following the roof replacement, the exterior stone facade was addressed. It is a sandstone in a very rough faced coursed ashlar configuration. The water table and trim details are smooth faced, to accent their significance. Over the years, the pointing had deteriorated and was missing or loose in many locations. The stones themselves had fared well, though there was specific locations of stone deterioration, mostly due to water damage. These occurred in locations where the roof had leaked or over run, or at the base of the building due to rising damp. This is the capillary action of ground water entering the stone and migrating upwards. Some areas of stone had to be patched using matching material, or in a few instances entire stones were replaced with matching details. At the tower the gargoyles had developed cracks. These had been previously secured with hook ties. The ties were replaced with stainless steel anchors to secure the sections of carved stone together. In other locations, lintels or sills or stone had cracked and stainless steel rods were installed to secure them.

The stone was cleaned using chemicals that are formulated for historic masonry. This was done to remove years of accumulated grime, dust, and coal residue, as well as the paint that had leached onto the stones from the roof. Test samples were completed to determine the concentration of chemicals, acceptable level of "clean" methods of application and time periods for application. These were observed for a period of time to insure the proper method was selected that would be a combination of clean stone without damage to the masonry or mortar.

left and below: roofing work on the Kanawha County Courthouse as part of their rehabilitation and maintenence efforts.

References: The County Courthouse, Michael Workman, Ph.D.

1 - This insight is shared by Donald R. Andrews, author of "County Government" in *The West Virginia Encyclopedia*, ed.,
    Ken Sullivan and Deborah J. Sonis, p. 173.
2 - Courthouses have traditionally served as ground zero in the measurement of distance between towns, a convention that continues
    today even on mile markers on our interstate highways.
3 - Lora A. Lamarre, "History of West Virginia Courthouses," WV Division of Culture and History, website, p. 1.
4 - National Association of Counties, "History of County Government, Part I, pp. 2-3, at www.wvaco.org; also Javersak,
    "Courthouses," p. 1, unpublished manuscript, July, 2009.
5 - Charles Henry Ambler, *West Virginia, The Mountain State*, New York: Prentice-Hall, Inc., 1940, pp. 68-69; National Association
    of Counties, "History of County Government," Part I, pp. 3-4.
6 - Ibid.; also quoted in Ambler, *West Virginia*, p. 70.
7 - bid.
8 - Chitwood, "Colonial Origins," pp. 441-42; Ambler, *West Virginia*, pp. 70-71.
9 - "Counties," in *The West Virginia Encyclopedia*, pp. 171-72.
10 - The full transcript of the trial is available online at "The Trial of John Brown," www.law.umkc.edu/faculty
11 - Brewer, "History of West Virginia Courthouses*, passim.*
12 - Brisbin, *West Virginia Politics and* Government, pp. 70-72; Brewer's report contains the language of Article VII, Section 1-5,
    which set up the township system, on pp. 2-3.
13 - David G. Temple, "Local Government Reorganization in West Virginia," *The West Virginia University Public Affairs Reporter*,
    Vol. 6, No. 3, 1989; also "Counties" in *The West Virginia Encyclopedia*, p. 171-7*2.*
14 - Brisbin, p. 75.
15 - National Association of Counties, 'The History of County Government," Part I, p. 5.
16 - Quoted in Brewer, "History of West Virginia Courthouses," p. 7.
17 - Robert Jay Dilger, "County Government in West Virginia," *The West Virginia University Public Affairs Reporter*, Vol. 15, No. 2
    (Spring, 1998).

Book References:

Our thanks to all those who provided the wealth of resources to this project. In additional to Michael Workman's bibliography, we
would also like to credit the Staff of the County Courthouses, Michael Gioulis, Historic Preservation Consultant, David T. Javersak,
Ph.D., and the many volunteers of West Virginia's County Historical and Genealogical Societies.

Bishop, William, H. 1927. History of Roane County, West Virginia. Spencer, WV: William H. Bishop.
Boone County, West Virginia, History. 1990. Madison, WV: Boone County Genealogical Society.
Cabell County Courthouse National Register of Historic Places Nomination. Rodney S. Collins (WVSHPO); Michael Pauley; and
    Michael Gioulis.
Caldwell, Nancy L. 1975. A History of Brooke County. Wellsburg, WV: Brooke County Historical Society.
Calhoun County Historical and Genealogical Society. 1989. History of Calhoun County, West Virginia. Waynesville, NC: Walsworth
    Publishing Company.
Clay County History Book Committee, 1989. History of Clay County, West Virginia, Clay, WV: Clay County History Book
    Committee.
Dayton, Ruth Woods. 1952. "The Beginning - Philippi, 1861." West Virginia History. July.
Doddridge County Bicentennial Commission. 1979. The History of Doddridge County, West Virginia. Dallas, TX: Taylor Publishing
    Corporation.
Doherty, William T. 1972. Berkeley County, U.S.A.: A Bicentennial History of a Virginia and West Virginia County, 1772-1972.
    Parsons, WV: McClain Printing Company, 1972.
Fayette County Chamber of Commerce. 1993. History of Fayette County, West Virginia. Oak Hill: Fayette County Chamber of
    Commerce.
Fayette County Courthouse National Register of Historic Places Nomination. James E. Harding. November 15, 1977.
Gilmer County Historical Society. 1994. History of Gilmer County, West Virginia, 1845-1989. Waynesville, NC: Walsworth
    Publishing Company.
Greenbrier County Courthouse and Lewis Spring National Register of Historic Places Nomination. C. Doyle Kester. May 12, 1972.
Jefferson County Courthouse National Register of Historic Places Nomination. Ted McGee. March 7, 1973.
Kanawha County Courthouse National Register of Historic Places Nomination. Rodney S. Collins. April 17, 1978.
Marion County Historical Society. A History of Marion County, West Virginia. Fairmont: MCHS, 1986.

Morton, Oren F. 1916. History of Monroe County, West Virginia. Dayton, VA: Ruebush-Elkins Company.

Morton, Oren F. 1914. A History of Preston County West Virginia. Kingwood, WV: The Journal Publishing Company.

Marshall County Historical Society. 1984. History of Marshall County, West Virginia. Salem: Walsworth Publishing.

Mercer County Courthouse National Register of Historic Places Nomination. Rodney S. Collins. July 14, 1980.

Monongalia County Courthouse National Register of Historic Places Nomination. Randall S. Gooden. January 17, 1985.

Pocahontas County Courthouse andJail National Register of Historic Places Nomination. Michael Gioulis. March 1, 1994.

Rice, Otis K. 1985. West Virginia: A History. Lexington, KY: The University of Kentucky Press.

Smith, Barbara. The Barbour County Courthouse. 2000.

Sullivan, Ken, Editor. The West Virginia Encyclopedia. West Virginia Humanities Council. 2006.

Sutton, John Davison. 1919. History of Braxton County and Central West Virginia. Parsons, WV: McClain Printing Company.

Tenney, Noel, Editor. 1993. All About Upshur County: A Bibliography and Resource Guide to the Published and Unpublished Materials About Upshur County, West Virginia. Buckhannon, West Virginia: Upshur County Historical Society.

Virgil A. Lewis. History of West Virginia, Philadelphia: Hubbard Brothers Publishers, 1889.

Wood County Courthouse National Register of Historic Places Nomination. Gary J. Tucker. March 11, 1978.

Wyoming County Courthouse and Jail National Register of Historic Places Nomination. Colonel C.E. Turley. October 25, 1978.

Photographic Resources

Alan Moats, Judge: 25 (top-right and top-right lower)

Barbara Smith: 24 (right-center)

Carole Menefee: 180 (bottom-right)

Christy Bailey: 111 (lower-left - R.D. Bailey)

Fairmont Landmarks Commission & MainStreet Fairmont: 93 (all)

Friends of Blackwater / J.R. Clifford Project: 163 (bottom-right – Supreme Court of Appeals)

Historic Beverly: 147 (center - defenders of Beverly)

Jeff Gentner: 29 (top and right-center); 30 (bottom-left); 38 (top); 44 (top); 47 (top); 89 (top and center-right); 90 (bottom – left and right); 98 (top); 104 (top); 107 (full); 110 (top); 113 (top); 122 (top); 137 (top); 139 (right-center and bottom-right); 155 (top); 182 (top – left); 184 (left-center)

Joseph Stiles – Historic Courthouses Postcard Collection: 36 (bottom); 39 (middle); 66 (upper); 69 (lower); 88 (top-left); 90 (top-right); 96 (all); 99 (top-right);102 (top-right);111 (left-center); 120 (top-left); 126 (all); 129 (center-right); 138 (bottom-left); 144 (bottom-left); 147 (bottom-center); 150 (top-left); 153 (center-left); 156 (bottom-left); 159 (center-right); 165 (top-right); 168 (top-left)

Ken Sherman: 61 (bottom-left)

Library of Congress: 57 (bottom-right); 79 (top-right); 132 (top-right and center); 174 (top-left); 177 (top-right); 183 (bottom-right)

Love Happiness Photography: 170 (lower-right);171 (right-center); 172 (lower-left)

Ludwig Family: 180 (upper left)

Marty Seufer: 184 (lower-left, lower-right, and lower-center)

Michael Gioulis: 117 (top-left);118 (center-right, center-left, bottom-right and bottom-left)

Michael Switzer: 116 (top); 117 (center-right); 158 (lower-right); 184 (top-left and center-right)

Morgan Messenger: 120 (bottom-right)

National Park Service: 163 (bottom-right)

Richard Lowe: 180 (lower-left, center-right)

Silling Associates, Inc.: 64 (upper-right); 85 (bottom-center); 142 (top-right); 145 (center-right)

Tucker County Historical Society: 162 (all)

Upshur County Historical Society: 169 (lower-right)

West Virginia State Archives: 91 (bottom-left); 111 (bottom-right)

WVU – West Virginia and Regional History Collection: 25 (top-left); 39 (top-left); 60 (center-left); 105 (top-left and bottom-left); 114 (top-left); 120 (center-right); 147 (top-right); 159 (top-left); 160 (lower-right); 183 (top-left and middle-left)

West Virginia's

Living Monuments

The Courthouses

A Project of the West Virginia Association of Counties

Documentary Video Sponsors

Platinum

West Virginia Courthouse Facilities
Improvement Authority

Diamond

BrickStreet
Chesapeake Energy
West Virginia Bar Foundation
West Virginia Humanities Council

Gold

Barbour County Commission
Casto & Harris
Coal Heritage Highway Authority
Kanawha County Commission
Marion County Commission
Marshall County Commission
Mercer County Commission
Randolph County Commission
Robinson & McElwee, PLLC
West Virginia Association of Circuit Clerks
West Virginia County Clerks' Association
West Virginia Counties Risk Pool
West Virginia Department of Education & the Arts
West Virginia Sheriffs' Association
Wood County Commission

Silver

ACS Computer Systems
Association of West Virginia Assessors
CSSI - Complete Systems Support, Inc.
Fayette County Commission
PPG
Pullin Fowler Flanagan Brown Poe, PLLC
Software Systems, Inc.
West Virginia Prosecuting Attorneys' Association
Wirt County Commission
Wyoming County Commission

The book is really an outgrowth of an earlier documentary project that focused on a selection of historic courthouses in the state. Given the one hour length of the production, there was not enough time to cover all the counties. There was a wave of requests for more information - more counties. In response, the book project was born. Our thanks again to all those who contributed their support to that project. It turned out to be a good investment as the production garnered an *Emmy* nomination and the *Spirit of West Virginia* award. Thanks again to all the sponsors and supporters of the documentary project.